THE

PEMBROKESHIRE

COAST

EXPLORING
THE
PEMBROKESHIRE
COAST

Phil Carradice

Parc Cenedlaethol Arfordir Penfro
Pembrokeshire Coast National Park

PUBLISHED AS A CONTRIBUTION TO CELEBRATE THE 50TH ANNIVERSARY OF
THE PEMBROKESHIRE COAST NATIONAL PARK IN 2002

First Impression – 2002

ISBN 1 84323 125 5

All photographs, unless otherwise stated, are owned and are
reproduced by kind permission of the Pembrokeshire Coast
National Park Authority. The publishers also gratefully
acknowledge the help and information provided by staff in
the Authority during the preparation of this book.

Preliminary photographs:
    Title page: Porth Clais
    Contents page: Skomer Island
    Introduction: Puffins (photo: Mike Edwards)

Printed in Wales at
Gomer Press, Llandysul, Ceredigion
gwasg@gomer.co.uk

In memory of my father, who taught
me to love and experience
The Pembrokeshire Coast.

P.C.

Contents

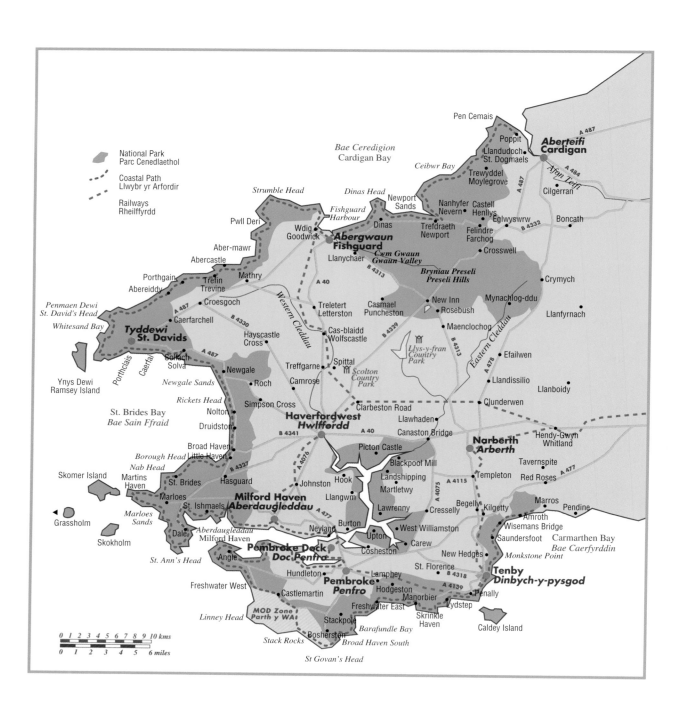

National Park
Parc Cenedlaethol

Coastal Path
Llwybr yr Arfordir

Railways
Rheilffyrdd

Pen Cemais

Bae Ceredigion
Cardigan Bay

Poppit
Llandudoch
St. Dogmaels
Aberteifi
Cardigan

Ceibwr Bay

Trewyddel
Moylegrove

Afon Teifi

A 487

A 484

Cilgerran

Strumble Head

Dinas Head

Newport
Sands

Nanhyfer
Nevern

Castell
Henllys

Eglwyswrw

Boncath

B 4332

Fishguard
Harbour

Pwll Deri

Wdig
Goodwick

Dinas

Trefdraeth
Newport

Felindre
Farchog

Crosswell

Aber-mawr

Abergwaun
Fishguard

Llanychaer

Cwm Gwaun
Gwaun Valley

Bryniau Preseli
Preseli Hills

Crymych

Abercastle

A 40

B 4313

New Inn
Rosebush

Mynachlog-ddu

Porthgain
Abereiddy

Trefin
Trevine

Mathry

Treletert
Letterston

Casmael
Puncheston

Maenclochog

Llanfyrnach

Croesgoch

A 487

B 4330

Caerfarchell

Cas-blaidd
Wolfscastle

B 4329

Penmaen Dewi
St. David's Head

Hayscastle
Cross

Llys-y-fran
Country
Park

Efailwen

Whitesand Bay

Tyddewi
St. Davids

Treffgarne

Spittal

Eastern Cleddau

Llandissilio

Llanboidy

A 478

B 4313

Western Cleddau

Scolton
Country
Park

Ynys Dewi
Ramsey Island

Solfach
Solva

Newgale

Roch

Camrose

Clunderwen

Newgale Sands

Porthclais

Caerfai

Rickets Head

Nolton

Simpson Cross

Clarbeston Road

Llawhaden

Hendy-Gwyn
Whitland

St. Brides Bay
Bae Sain Ffraid

Druidston

Haverfordwest
Hwlffordd

Canaston Bridge

Narberth
Arberth

B 4341

A 40

Broad Haven

Borough Head Little Haven

Picton Castle

Tavernspite

Nab Head

B 4327

A 4076

Blackpool Mill

Templeton

Red Roses

A 477

Skomer Island

Martins
Haven

St. Brides

Hasguard

Johnston

Hook

Landshipping

Martletwy

A 4115

Begelly

Kilgetty

Marros

Pendine

Marloes

Llangwm

A 4075

Cressely

Amroth

Marloes
Sands

St. Ishmaels

Milford Haven
Aberdaugleddau

Lawrenny

West Williamston

Wisemans Bridge

Grassholm

Skokholm

Dale

Aberdaugleddau
Milford Haven

Neyland

Burton

A 477

Upton

Coshesten

Carew

Saundersfoot

Carmarthen Bay
Bae Caerfyrddin

New Hedges

Monkstone Point

St. Ann's Head

Angle

Pembroke Dock
Doc Penfro

St. Florence

B 4318

Tenby
Dinbych-y-pysgod

Hundleton

Pembroke
Penfro

Lamphey

Hodgeston

A 4139

Penally

Freshwater West

Castlemartin

Freshwater East

Manorbier

Tydstep

Linney Head

MOD Zone
Parth y WA

Stackpole

Skrinkle
Haven

Caldey Island

Bosherston

Barafundle Bay

Stack Rocks

Broad Haven South

St Govan's Head

0 1 2 3 4 5 6 7 8 9 10 kms

0 1 2 3 4 5 6 miles

Introduction

The county of Pembrokeshire is dominated by the sea. Water stretches around three sides of its land mass and there is nowhere in the county that is more than a dozen or so miles from the coast. It is inevitable, therefore, that the sea – more than anything else – has helped to shape the character of the people in this, the westernmost point of Wales, and the very land on which they live.

Soaring sea cliffs and long golden beaches are the trademark of Pembrokeshire. They are deservedly renowned with visitors and armchair travellers alike. Yet there is a lot more here for people to see and enjoy. Above all, the sense of history is profound in Pembrokeshire. Look at a map of the county and you will see that it is virtually a mirror image of the larger outline of Wales. In its shape, in its history, in its topography and geology, Pembrokeshire is almost a microcosm. As such it encapsulates much of the story of Wales.

Ancient monuments, standing stones and cromlechs, Norman castles and Iron Age fortresses abound; there is industrial archaeology in the shape of coalmines, iron works and a Royal Naval Dockyard; the wildlife of the county is stunning in its range and variety – from sea birds and seals to falcons and rare choughs. Everything a visitor could ever want is available here: seaside resorts like Tenby and Saundersfoot or the quiet solemnity of the Pembrokeshire Coast Path.

Pembrokeshire is Britain's only coastal National Park. Its superb scenery – including islands like Skomer and Ramsey – make it a unique experience for anyone who ventures to the west of Wales. Above all, this is a timeless and untroubled part of the world where relaxation and the cultural enjoyment on offer are second to none.

There are many ways to experience the best of Pembrokeshire. The Coast Path, 186 miles (299 km) in length, is undoubtedly one of the most stunning walks in Britain. Yet you don't need to tramp along its full length – drop in and drop out as you choose. Having said that, there are some sections that should not be missed and you can, after all, only see so much from the comfort of your car.

Being a native of south Pembrokeshire, rather than the more Welsh-speaking north of the county, I tend to use the English form of place-names. So that readers may see two languages at work side by side, a bilingual list of place-names is provided at the back of this book.

The Pembrokeshire coast is one of the most spectacular regions of Britain. It deserves to be visited and enjoyed. Perhaps equally as important, it should be recollected in tranquillity – as Wordsworth once said. And that applies even if you've never been within a hundred miles of the place.

Enjoy this book. Then put it to one side and go and explore the area for yourself. You won't be disappointed.

PHIL CARRADICE, 2002

vii

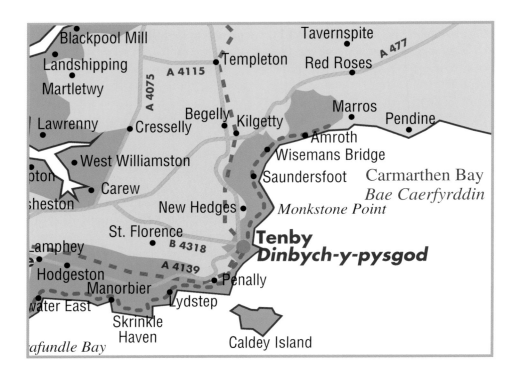

Chapter One

Amroth to Manorbier

EVEN in high season, when the countryside is full of eager holidaymakers, there is a remoteness, a majestic sense of isolation about the Pembrokeshire coast. In winter, when knife-sharp westerly winds whip in off the sea, you could easily find yourself the only human being anywhere in view – on beach, cliff path, village or town. Wherever you are on the two-hundred-mile length of coast, whatever the season or weather, the sense of being separate and alone, of everything being somehow different, is all pervasive.

In the south, the Pembrokeshire coast begins at the village of Amroth. Just a few miles to the east lies Pendine – which, while it is not Pembrokeshire itself, is always a popular spot with Pembrokeshire people. It was on Pendine's rock-hard sands that the World Land Speed Record was broken five times in the late 1920s. When J G Parry Thomas was killed on 3rd March 1927, trying to reclaim the record from Malcolm Campbell, they buried his car Babs on the beach as a mark of respect.

For years harassed parents claimed themselves an hour or two of precious peace by telling their children to go off and dig for the car. Then, in the last part of the twentieth century, officialdom stepped in and rescued Babs from her sandy grave. She now goes on show each summer at Pendine Museum. It might be a positive, even a welcome move, but for those who used to dig fruitlessly for the relic it seems that some of the fun disappeared from the sands the day that Babs was taken away.

Further west, within the boundaries of Pembrokeshire, is the village of Amroth which clings precariously to the coastline. 'Clings' is the operative word here as the area has suffered dramatically from coastal erosion over the years. The beach is wide, however, and in the summer the bathing is excellent.

At the furthest extremity of the beach, beyond the low-water mark – only visible on a very low tide – lies a submerged forest. The ancient woodland was overwhelmed by rising sea levels at the end of the Ice Age. If you're lucky enough to ever see it, stand for a moment or two and gaze at the ancient peat and tree stumps. Remember that you're touching history, staring at something which was alive and breathing six or seven thousand years ago.

The view across Jack Sound towards the low squat bulk of SKOMER ISLAND

1

The beach at AMROTH, start of the Coast Path and the southern end of the Landsker

Remember also the old Welsh legend of Cantre'r Gwaelod. The story is a famous one. A local prince was holding a feast and one unfortunate sentry, whose duty it was to close the sluice gates at the end of the day – thus keeping out the ever-encroaching ocean – was too eager to consume his share of wine. He left the gates open and flood water poured in over the palace, forest and unsuspecting people. The truth may be more prosaic, of course, but it's not nearly so attractive as the fiction.

Amroth developed as a mining village, tapping in on the rich seam of anthracite – it is after all at the western extremity of the South Wales Coalfield – which runs out into the sea at this point. Just inland, at places like Kilgetty and Reynaldson, you will find the remains of old colliery workings, a reminder that this whole area once had visions of grandeur and wealth to rival even the Rhondda valley. Together with nearby Wiseman's Bridge and Saundersfoot, Amroth prospered in the 'coal rush' days of the early Industrial Revolution. It's hard to believe but in 1801 this was the most densely populated parish in Pembrokeshire. Time was you could literally dig for coal on the beach here in Amroth. How things change.

The history of the village goes back a lot further than the Industrial Revolution, however. A small motte-and-bailey castle was built here by one of the knights who accompanied Arnulf de Montgomery to Pembroke in 1093. Despite this, you won't find much here in the way of remains. Located near the village church, the place rarely rates a mention in books about Welsh castles but it is important all the same because it marks the southernmost end of the Landsker, that invisible but highly significant line of demarcation which runs across the broad belly of Pembrokeshire. Since the coming of the Normans in

A section of the Coast Path showing one of the many gullies and clefts in the rocks

the late eleventh century the Landsker has divided the county into two – an Englishry, known as Little England, to the south; and a Welshry to the north. It is, in fact, a frontier, marked by a regular string of motte-and-bailey castles like Hayscastle, Maenclochog and Henry's Moat. In later years these were superseded by strong stone castles such as Llawhaden, Narberth and Roch which sat just inside the Landsker. It is a mysterious line of separation which, in its own way, was as effective as Hadrian's Wall in the north of England.

Once they had established a foothold in west Wales, the Normans engaged on an effective policy of transplantation, moving the native Welsh out of the Englishry and bringing in their own settlers to the fertile lands of the south. The divide is a clear one. As late as Elizabethan times the Pembrokeshire writer George Owen was describing villages where those who spoke Welsh and those who spoke English were divided by little more than the width of a pathway or street. The differences these days may not be so clear-cut but you can still trace the Landsker line across the county and the two peoples of Pembrokeshire still retain their own individual characters.

In the fourteenth century the Normans built a more substantial stone castle at Amroth, replacing the early motte-and-bailey fortress. This, too, has largely disappeared, having fallen prey to the wind and to the landowners of the district who eagerly carried away the stones to build their own houses once the castle fell into disrepair. All that now remains is a single gateway, but even that has undergone extensive repairs and bears little resemblance to the original structure. A modern house stands on the site of the castle, now part of a holiday complex of caravans and chalets. In the summer the place is full of tourists and day-trippers and the original, warlike nature of Amroth has been long forgotten.

Wiseman's Bridge lies only a few miles along the coast from Amroth. Just inland is the quiet village of Stepaside. It may be quiet now but in the eighteeth century the large iron works of The Pembrokeshire Iron and Coal Company stood here – in fact the remains of an old tramway, to the west of Sardis Mountain, can still be seen. This was part of the rail link from the network of coalmines around Kilgetty to the harbour at Saundersfoot – long gone now but the memories remain. The iron works opened in 1849, using anthracite coal from the Grove Colliery. For several years over 4,000 tons of pig iron was exported annually through nearby Saundersfoot but production ceased in 1877.

It is said that Churchill and Eisenhower came to Wiseman's Bridge to watch rehearsals for the D Day landings on the beach in August 1943. Known as Operation Jantzen, the rehearsals took place between 22nd July and 5th August. However, there are doubts about the presence of the two 'big men' in Pembrokeshire at that time.

In late July 1943 Churchill is recorded as being in London and at Chequers; then, in early August, he set off for a conference in Quebec. Eisenhower, at the time, was in Italy and had yet to be appointed supreme commander for the invasion of France. So their attendance at Wiseman's Bridge is doubtful.

An old tunnel, originally built for the rail link from the Kilgetty and Stepaside coalmines to Saundersfoot, takes you from the western end of Wiseman's Bridge to Saundersfoot, the first of the large – or largish – towns on the coast. There is an alternative route along the cliff top but the romance

The old tunnel between WISEMAN'S BRIDGE and SAUNDERSFOOT

and intrigue of the railway draws most people towards the tunnel. Stand, if you can, at the entrance to the tunnel for a while and admire the skill of the men who excavated this long hole in the rock. Pitch-black and echoing, this is a stunning piece of engineering. You can see an arch of white light ahead of you as you walk into the gloom, then you burst out into the sunshine with the village and port of Saundersfoot waiting for you ahead.

There is an ancient tale, told in these parts, about an old couple who operated as wreckers at Amroth and Wiseman's Bridge several hundred years ago. Their only son left home and went off to seek his fortune. Then one night, hearing of a vessel beating in from the Atlantic, the old couple set their false lights and settled down in front of their fire as the ship died on the rocks below.

The following morning, gleefully sifting through the debris on the beach, the old man came across the half-drowned body of a sailor at the water's edge. There could be no survivors. Taking a large stone he quickly smashed in the sailor's skull. When he turned over the body to search the dead man's pockets, he was appalled to see the face of his only son.

It is indeed a great story. Unfortunately, you'll also hear exactly the same tale about St Donats in the Vale of Glamorgan – and probably many other parts of Wales as well.

Saundersfoot owes its existence to coal. The 'black gold' was brought down to this tiny port either by rail or by horse and cart from nearby collieries like Jeffreyston and Coppet Hall. The harbour was finished in 1834 and by the 1880s nearly 100,000 tons of coal were being exported annually across its docks and quays. The railway line ran along the edge of the sea and even down the main street of the town. You can still find old photographs of the 'Miners' Express' in antique shops or the stocks of specialist postcard dealers, showing open carriages or carts full of colliers being transported up and down the street. However, by the beginning of the Second World War the bubble had burst, the collieries were closed and the town faced a bleak future.

Salvation came in the shape of the tourist industry. Despite the mainline station being located a mile or so inland, Saundersfoot's fine beach and safe bathing made it an ideal holiday location once paid leave became an accepted way of life after 1945.

Visitors should try not to miss seeing the anticline. This semi-circular pattern in the rock strata on the shore, just north of the tunnel from Wiseman's Bridge, shows where an upfold in the rocks has been cut through by erosion. It's a fascinating geological phenomenon and is only visible at low tide.

The variety of rocks found in Pembrokeshire is exceptionally wide ranging. Put simply, the headlands on this coast are made up of hard rock

The harbour at SAUNDERSFOOT, once a major coal port, now a peaceful marina and yachting basin

South Beach at TENBY, one of the most popular holiday locations in Wales

while the bays consist of softer varieties and show where erosion and the working of the sea have cut into the shoreline. Here in the south of the county you will find the youngest rocks, geologically speaking.

The range is vast – Carboniferous Limestone, Old Red Sandstone and, in the Tenby/Saundersfoot area, Millstone Grit. This latter rock crumbles and falls on a regular basis. There's been a lot of stabilising of the cliff faces around here, with netting being pinned up on the most dangerous surfaces. Even so, a serious rock fall closed the old railway tunnel at Wiseman's Bridge and part of the Coast Path in 1980. Even now care needs to be taken, particularly in the winter months.

Monkstone Point, effectively the dividing headland between Saundersfoot and Tenby, has a small islet, just 48 feet high, perched off its easternmost point. The islet first appeared on Saxton's map of 1578 and careful exploration indicates that there may once have been a beacon store or even a religious cell on the top of it.

In Welsh, Tenby is known as Dinbych-y-pysgod, which means 'the little fort of fishes'. The place is well named, as the harbour and the castle ruins dominate the town. It is a spectacularly beautiful walled town with two of the best beaches in west Wales.

The original Norman castle dates from the twelfth century; its capture by the Lord Rhys in 1152 is the first recorded mention of the place. Apparently the Welsh leader and his brother Maelgwyn came over the sands from Amroth and took the defenders by surprise. A stone castle was erected on the headland overlooking the harbour in the thirteenth century.

The town and castle were subjected to bombardment from the forces of Parliamentarian General Roland Laugharne during the English Civil War. Ships moored off the coast also contributed to the battering but it was only after the untimely death of Governor Gwynne that the fortress surrendered.

Later, during the Second Civil War, Tenby declared for the King, and Oliver Cromwell himself appeared outside its walls. Leaving his deputy, Colonel Horton, to continue the siege, Cromwell rode on to Pembroke. At the end of May 1648 Colonel Rice Powell surrendered to the Parliamentarians and that effectively marked the end of Tenby's military history.

For many years this was a working port, fishing and the export of coal being the main industries. Fishing is still carried on but these days it is a low-key affair with a dozen or so boats operating out of the tidal harbour. For nearly two hundred years the town has survived largely on tourism.

The area around the harbour remains particularly atmospheric. Laston House, situated right on the harbour, was the site of the old Sea Water Baths and

5

The harbour at TENBY

Assembly Rooms for the town. They were built by Sir William Paxton in 1811, the idea being to turn Tenby into a seaside version of Bath or Cheltenham. And for a while it worked. The motto 'The Sea Washes Away All the Ills of Man' – in Greek, of course – is still emblazoned over the door of Laston House.

Yet what many visitors don't realise is that this building later played host to one of the early pioneers of the photographer's art. Charles Smith Allen moved here from Lichfield, Staffordshire, in the 1860s and set up his studio in Laston House where a complicated system of shutters and blinds helped to control the light into the studio. Allen's photographic views of Tenby and the surrounding area are now highly prized – as are those of his son S J Allen, who soon established his own business in nearby Pembroke Dock.

The nationalisation of the coalmines at the end of the Second World War brought holidays with pay, for the first time in British history. And with the advent of mass tourism, 'miners' fortnight' and the like, Tenby really came into its own as a holiday destination. Hotels, guesthouses and caravan parks proliferated. Campbell's steamers – the famous White Funnel Fleet – had been calling at the port for many years before that, however.

Royal Victoria Pier was built on the seaward side of Castle Hill by the Borough Council, with some private assistance, between 1897 and 1899. This meant that paddle steamers could take on and discharge passengers at almost every stage of the tide. The pier was poorly maintained, however, and in the late 1940s it was demolished. From then on the steamers had to dock at the harbour on the landward side of the hill. The port was tidal and the decline of

Tenby as one of the White Funnel Fleet destinations coincided with the general demise of large-ship cruising on the Bristol Channel. Now the place is left to the fishing boats and the small pleasure cruisers which take visitors out to Caldey Island and around the coast.

Tenby Museum was founded in the 1870s and has to be one of the best small museums you will ever find. Located in the old castle ruins, this superb establishment has an extensive library and an excellent collection of paintings by Augustus and Gwen John.

Augustus and Gwen were born in the town, of course, and lived there for some years. There is a wonderful tale about the shy, conventional Augustus going bathing in the summer of 1897 on Tenby's North Beach. Apparently he dived in and hit his head on a rock. The accident led to a dramatic reversal of his character and the bohemian, brawling, extrovert genius was born. It's probably apocryphal but it would be good to find at least a degree of truth in the tale.

The path out of Tenby takes you around the MOD firing range at Penally and part of the town's famous golf club. Founded in 1888, this is the oldest golf course in Wales. However, with a recorded instance of the town mayor adjourning his court 13 years earlier in order to play a game of golf on the dunes outside the town, the history of the game at Tenby obviously dates back even further.

Trefloyne Golf Club lies close to the original Tenby course and was the scene of a bloody battle during the English Civil War. Roland Laugharne – the same Roland Laugharne who besieged the town of Tenby – battered down the walls of Trefloyne House in February 1644. His 'army', consisting of 300 foot soldiers, 50 horse and several pieces of heavy artillery, made short work of the walls and the house has now disappeared. Golfers searching for lost golf balls in the woods adjacent to the course may find the occasional bit of rubble but that is all that now remains of the Royalist stronghold.

From Giltar Point there is a wonderful view of the nearby islands. Most visitors to the area don't realise that there are actually two offshore islands here – Caldey and St Margaret's. Caldey is famous for its monks who first came here in the sixth century. Their settlement was short lived, however, as raiding Viking marauders and pirates soon wiped them out. Not to be intimidated, further groups of holy men soon made their homes on the island and battled against the elements and the sea raiders in order to create their settlement.

The Old Priory and St Illtud's church were built on the site of the original community in about 1113, probably by Benedictine Monks from St Dogmaels in Ceredigion. The island was bought by the Revd W Dorre Bushell in 1897 and the present monastery, with its elegant Romanesque features, was created some 15 years later.

As far as possible, the monks remain self-sufficient, living and farming alongside the 60 or so inhabitants of the island. Farming on Caldey has always been hard as winter gales sweep in unchecked across the flat surface – 180 feet at its highest point. A lighthouse was built there in 1828, high above Chapel Point on the east coast. Now automatic, it was once operated by three lighthouse keepers. It would have been a lonely existence. These days the island receives thousands of visitors during the summer months, with boats from Tenby taking trippers out to enjoy the magnificent cliff scenery, the beaches and the monastery gardens.

The cliffs at LYDSTEP with the low shape of Caldey Island in the background

Flowers galore – at times the cliff tops are a riot of glorious colour

St Margaret's lies off the western tip of Caldey. Only 14 acres in size, the island is home to breeding cormorants and boasts some of the most spectacular cliff scenery on the whole of the Pembrokeshire coast. They used to quarry limestone here in the nineteenth century but it must have been one of the most god-forsaken spots in the whole world to live and work. Today, there is no public access to the island.

Lydstep Head provides a superb example of soaring limestone cliffs. Here you will find rock beds which, 290 million years ago, were upended into vertical positions when the continents collided. The rock formations can be identified in the shapes of

beach is in private hands but you can still explore the caverns at low tide.

Skrinkle Haven lies just beyond Lydstep. For many years this bay was out of bounds, when the Royal Artillery camp at nearby Manorbier was in full swing. Now the beach is open again and is well worth a visit, either in summer or winter.

A narrow strip of limestone, known locally as the Church Doors (due to several huge cave entrances in the rock) divides Skrinkle Haven into two – sandy beach on one side, rocky cove on the other. This is the point where the limestone ends and Old Red Sandstone takes over. It means that the cliffs are

SKRINKLE HAVEN with the long nose of the Church Doors cutting the bay in two.

the outcrops or pinnacles, which are interwoven by inlets formed along the fault lines. Being rich in calcium, limestone grasslands like this are home to hundreds of wild flowers. As the headland has been owned by the National Trust since 1936, there has been little or no use of artificial fertilisers or pesticides and here you can find plants and flowers like thick gorse, knapweed, kidney vetch and carline thistle. In the summer the cliff top can be a riot of colour.

The village of Lydstep lies inland. Built primarily by the first viscount St Davids, the village has been overshadowed by the famous Lydstep Caverns. The

King's Quoit at MANORBIER on the south coast

unstable and flaky so you need to take care where you walk or climb.

King's Quoit, a Neolithic burial chamber some 5,000 years old, lies just outside the village of Manorbier and is one of those superb monuments which are best seen in the early evening if you want to obtain maximum spiritual effect.

The castle at Manorbier must have one of the most atmospheric views in the whole of Wales, being situated halfway up the hill overlooking a narrow stretch of golden beach. The vagaries of war largely passed Manorbier by and so it remains very much as it must have looked, back in the thirteenth century.

The castle is most famous as being the birthplace, in 1146, of Giraldus Cambrensis. After St Paul he was probably one of the first travel writers in the world, producing seventeen books, including the wonderful *Journey Through Wales*, but failing to achieve his ultimate ambition – to become the bishop of St Davids. Giraldus, a Norman – albeit with a lot of Welsh blood in his veins – called Manorbier 'the pleasantest spot in Wales.'

The few wax figures scattered around the castle walls and chambers – presumably representing Giraldus and his family – are some of the most unrealistic dummies you're ever likely to see. Still, you can't have everything and the sight of the sun setting over the hills and the quiet sea rippling up onto the beach will more than compensate for their lifelessness.

MANORBIER Castle, birthplace of Giraldus Cambrensis

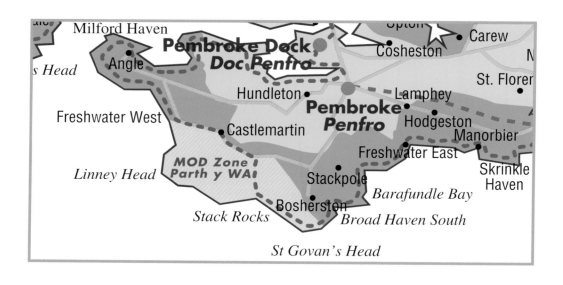

Chapter Two:

Manorbier to Angle

THE stretch of coast from Manorbier to Angle must surely be the most remote yet also the most rugged part of the whole Pembrokeshire experience. There are no towns, the largest human gatherings being tiny seasonal places like Freshwater East or the village of Angle.

The scenery is majestic, a mixture of huge limestone cliffs which soar upwards to the sky and the multi-coloured mud and silt of Old Red Sandstone. The range and variety of bird life is exceptional, everything from guillemots and puffins to oystercatchers and, if you are lucky, the rare chough.

Heading westwards from Manorbier it is all too easy to miss beautiful Swanlake Bay. Access to this deserted strip of sand and shingle is along the clearly marked Pembrokeshire Coast Path but you need to take care as there are dozens of fissures in the rock. The beach at Swanlake is rarely used and in summer this is the ideal place to lie back, relax and put the world to rights – in your head, of course.

Freshwater East is different, having long been a popular spot with holidaymakers. At the end of the nineteenth century wealthy middle-class tradesmen from nearby Pembroke and Pembroke Dock built themselves crude summer bungalows on the sand dunes which stretch up for several hundred feet behind the beach. These were mostly corrugated tin shacks but over the years many of them have been modified into substantial residences which are now in use all year round.

The 1950s brought caravan parks to Freshwater East, as well as the tents of hardy campers who braved the elements and the proliferation of adders and glow worms which haunted the dunes. In the 1970s a holiday village was created on the south-western side of the bay. Sadly, overuse of the dunes has led directly to a decrease in the adder population and to significant damage to the dunes themselves. The National Park Authority is in the process of developing plans to replant and restore the dune grasslands and the flanking woods. This will not only improve opportunities for wildlife to breed and live but also give visitors and locals the chance for access.

Like many of the beaches on this part of the coast, Freshwater East was once a popular location for smugglers to land their ill-gotten gains. An air of

The magnificent cliff scenery of PEMBROKESHIRE – a typical view

STACKPOLE QUAY

romance still surrounds the ancient art of smuggling. The essayist Charles Lamb once declared, 'I like a smuggler. He is the only honest thief.' His views were undoubtedly tainted by the attitudes of people in the seventeenth and eighteenth centuries when many of the luxuries in life were denied to ordinary folk by high import taxes and by a genuine shortage of desirable goods. Small wonder, then, that Rudyard Kipling was later able to gleefully write:

> Five and twenty ponies
> Trotting through the dark –
> Brandy for the parson,
> 'Baccy for the Clerk;
> Laces for a lady, letters for a spy,
> And watch the wall, my darling, while the Gentlemen go by!

heard that a smuggling gang was unloading a cargo of illicit spirits on the beach at Freshwater. Unarmed but determined, he and three helpers immediately rode to the beach to apprehend them.

The smugglers fled when they saw the horsemen. Having secured the casks of brandy, Cawdor and his companions turned for home. At that point the smugglers returned, two boatloads of them this time. Cawdor and his men were attacked by a band of desperate villains, the smugglers using cudgels and heavy metal pokers in their assault. Cawdor was beaten to the ground but with great strength and courage he fought back to his feet and his assailants fled.

One of the smugglers was captured and taken to a house at nearby Trewent. Yet the adventure was not over, as Lady Caroline Cawdor later recorded in a letter to Charles Greville of Milford –

FRESHWATER EAST beach, scene of a dramatic fight with smugglers in the nineteenth century

Reality, however, was very different. Smugglers were invariably vicious criminals who were intent only on making a swift fortune for themselves. One story concerning smugglers, the beach at Freshwater East and Lord Cawdor is worth recounting.

Cawdor was the local landlord, living at nearby Stackpole Court, and was the man who defeated the invading French when they landed at Fishguard in 1797. Four years later, in November 1801, Cawdor

'A short time after, the house was surrounded by about thirty of the gang, people of the country armed with bludgeons, who immediately rescued their comrade. Warrants are out for apprehending those men that are known but none are as yet taken.'

Clearly, then, smuggling gangs were not the warm-hearted romantic rogues of popular legend.

Trewent Point, to the south-west of Freshwater, is the first of several striking headlands which reach out like giant fingers into the sea on this stretch of the coast. A little further west, at Greenala Point, you can walk through the ramparts and defensive banks of an ancient promontory fort. This Iron Age fortress was an elaborate and powerful defence work, one of many similar monuments to be found on the headlands around Pembrokeshire. It made sense. The steep cliff sides would have provided excellent natural defences against assault and while it is likely that most people would normally have lived outside the walls, promontory forts like this one would have provided a substantial degree of safety to retreat to once danger threatened.

Greenala Point sits heavily impressive in the water, its sides and rocks layered with bright orange lichens. It creates a majestic and striking sight when caught by the bright morning sun.

A little further along the coast you will find Stackpole Quay. The tiny harbour was built in the late eighteenth century, in order to export limestone from a nearby quarry. A secondary task for the port,

but one that was almost as vital, was to bring in luxury goods for the Cawdors at Stackpole Court, a few miles inland. Stackpole Court has been demolished now but was once a substantial house with over 300 rooms. The quay at Stackpole, Bosherston Lily Ponds and the nearby beach of Barafundle remain as a lasting tribute to the Cawdor family and their long-gone way of life.

These days the quarry at Stackpole Quay is an outdoor pursuits centre while the harbour is just a tidal backwater. In legend, Bosherston Lily Ponds were supposedly the body of water where King Arthur was given his sword Excalibur by the Lady in the Lake. However, the modern ponds were created at the end of the eighteenth century when the Cawdors dammed three limestone valleys, thus making a series of artificial lakes.

The National Trust took over much of the Stackpole estate in 1977 and the 80 acres of the ponds are now home to a wide range of wildlife such as otters, water fowl and dragonflies. The water

BOSHERSTON Lily Ponds – did King Arthur lurk here?

lilies bloom in June and early July and are an impressive sight as you walk alongside the lakes and the stream which feeds them, down to the beach at Broad Haven. The walk is one of carefully constructed elegance, in contrast to the rugged grandeur experienced on most of this coast.

It's hardly surprising. The pathway, like the lily ponds, was created by the Cawdors in the eighteenth century, that age of elegance and reason when learned and well-educated ladies and gentlemen would solemnly close the blinds of carriages rather than see raw nature in the wild.

The Cawdors were an interesting family. Alexander Campbell, heir to the Cawdor estates and castle in Scotland, had been at Cambridge with Gilbert Lort at the end of the seventeenth century. It was often quicker for young Campbell to travel home by going west to Lort's house at Stackpole and then to take a ship from there to Scotland. On one occasion he found himself storm-bound at Stackpole for some weeks. Romance between Alexander and Lort's sister Elizabeth quickly blossomed and the Cawdor family came to west Wales.

The most famous member of the Cawdor family, of course, was John Campbell, the man who fought the smugglers at Freshwater East and the French at Fishguard. Elevated to the peerage in 1796, he had already represented Cardigan in Parliament for 18 years and was popularly known as Squire Campbell. He ran his 16,000-acre estate as a progressive model landowner and agriculturalist. Tall and commanding Cawdor raised a troop of Yeomanry Cavalry during the French Revolutionary Wars, the simple beginnings of what would later become the Pembrokeshire Yeomanry.

BARAFUNDLE BAY, deserted and idyllic on the south coast

A spectacular blow hole, BOSHERSTON MERE during a gale in 1935

15

Barafundle Bay used to be a private beach for the Cawdors, situated well away from the public on one of the quieter parts of the Stackpole estate. There is still no road access to the beach and you have to walk over the cliff tops to reach the golden sands. It is well worth the walk. If you look carefully you will see the ruined remains of colonnades which once lined the path and the steps down to the beach – another example of Cawdor delicacy and designs of grandeur.

The vertical cliffs of Stackpole Head divide Barafundle Bay from Broad Haven. The headland is well known as a breeding ground for kittiwakes, razorbills and guillemots but here you will also find blow holes, places where cave roofs have collapsed to form deep holes in the rock. On storm-lashed days you might be lucky enough to witness the spectacular sight of spray and foam spouting upwards through these apertures, a bizarre but fascinating experience.

Broad Haven (these days known as Broad Haven South to distinguish it from the other Broad Haven, north of the Cleddau) is one of the finest of all Pembrokeshire strands. A stream runs down to the beach, draining out of the nearby lily ponds, and off-shore lies a strangely menacing limestone stack known as Church Rock. It's dramatically shaped, not unlike the religious edifice after which it is named,

and is invariably a draw to daredevil swimmers. Beware, however, the rock is further away than you think and the water around its base is dark and cold. Much better to sit on the beach and take in the view. The dunes are full of marram grass and wild flowers like bindweed and ragwort. They will repay your attention far better than Church Rock.

From this point onwards the coastal scenery becomes increasingly dramatic. The rocks here are limestone and the action of the waves has produced a proliferation of sea caves, blow holes and natural arches.

The superbly atmospheric chapel of St Govan's is tucked into the foot of the sea cliff a few miles south of Bosherston village. Local tradition asks you to count the number of roughly hewn steps on your way down to the chapel – it's never the same number when you count them climbing back up.

Although the chapel itself dates from the fourteenth century its foundation and origins remain unclear. One theory states that St Govan was really Sir Gawain of King Arthur fame. He became, people claim, a hermit after the death of his beloved king. The area has several Arthurian connections so the tale may have at least a grain of truth about it.

More probably St Govan was really Gobhan, an Irish priest and hermit who came to south Pembrokeshire in the sixth century. The chapel is

The beach at BROAD HAVEN SOUTH

16

The tiny chapel of St Govan's, isolated and atmospheric on the Pembrokeshire coast

well hidden, both from the land and sea, and would have been an ideal location for a holy man who was trying to lock himself away from the world. Hiding from sea raiders was not always easy, however. A famous tale tells how St Govan was once forced to hide from marauding pirates in a narrow cleft in the rock, close to the altar in the present chapel. The rock apparently opened up to allow him to conceal himself, then closed around his body to keep him totally secure. Once the pirates had left, the rock conveniently opened up to allow St Govan back out. The markings on the rock, it is claimed, are the imprint of his ribs! Stand in the cleft today, says the legend, make a wish before you turn around and the wish will come true.

Below the chapel, close to the point where waves lap against the rocks, is a holy well. This was supposed to counter rheumatism and lameness and, in the Middle Ages, thousands of pilgrims came here each year in an attempt to cure their ailments. In an arch above the chapel a bell once hung. Often it sounded without the help of any human – the signal for death or disaster at sea.

The section of the Pembrokeshire Coast Path between St Govan's Head and Stack Rocks is ideal for mountain biking and walking but the nearby MOD firing ranges at Castlemartin sometimes cause

it to be closed for access. The ranges were established in 1939, just prior to the outbreak of the Second World War. Even when the path is open you are well advised to stick to the beaten track as unexploded shells and bombs are often found on the ranges.

Huntsman's Leap is a dramatic fault in the rock, a narrow but deep chasm which cuts across the cliff top just before Saddle Head. Formed by sea erosion along a fault line (officially known as a 'geo') it can be reached by walking westwards from St Govan's Chapel. The story of Huntsman's Leap is known by all Pembrokeshire schoolchildren – a huntsman once leapt the gap only to die of a heart attack when he got off his horse and paused to look down into the terrifying depths of the chasm.

The sheer limestone cliffs on this section of coast are ideal for rock climbing. There is an excellent range of routes, everything from easy scrambles to extreme climbs which will test even the most experienced of climbers. Most of the routes are very exposed and this, combined with the stunning views, means that here you will find some of the best sea-cliff climbing in Britain. There are 'climbing seasons', however, so as not to interfere with breeding birds, for example. The cliffs of Carboniferous Limestone are around 350 millions years old and are the regular haunt of cormorants, fulmars and razorbills.

Inset: Chough (drawing by Fran Evans)

The rugged south coast

A few miles inland lies Merrion Camp. For many years this was the base for visiting German troops and tanks. The German army first came to the area in the 1950s, returning every summer to stay at Merrion and train on the adjacent Castlemartin ranges. Only comparatively recently have the visits ceased. The ranges are still used by British troops, however, as well as by other NATO forces, and the gates to Merrion Camp are still marked by two veteran tanks, named Romulus and Remus.

To the west of Merrion a single-track road runs you back to the cliff top and to Stack Rocks – or, to give them their correct name, Elegug Stacks. This pair of huge rock pillars stand just offshore. They were once part of a natural arch, formed when the sea cut through a narrow headland. The actual arch or top section collapsed long ago, leaving only the two splendid stacks isolated out in the sea.

Close to Stack Rocks lies the Green Bridge of Wales, a huge arch through which the sea boils and foams in constant fury. This whole area, including the Green Bridge and Stack Rocks, provides a home for tens of thousands of sea birds such as razorbills and guillemots. It's easy to see how Stack Rocks got their name – elegug is Viking for guillemot. If you are lucky you might even spot rare choughs and peregrines along this stretch of coast.

The MOD ranges cover a large part of the land here and access is prohibited. Walkers (or car drivers) have to retrace their steps down the road towards Merrion Camp at this point. This road, incidentally, passes Flimston Church which has stood unscathed in the middle of the ranges for many years. Until 1960 its windows were boarded up but the building has now been fully restored and church services are sometimes held there.

STACK ROCKS, seen from the air

The village of Castlemartin, once a fortified hilltop camp, boasts what has to be the oldest traffic roundabout in Britain. The eighteenth-century cattle pound which lies at the eastern end of the village has become a convenient way of controlling vehicles approaching from four separate directions – pragmatism at its best!

Castlemartin Church lies to the north, secluded and atmospheric. A series of steps leads you to the altar of this beautiful little church where the organ is reputed to have once belonged to the composer Mendelssohn.

A short car drive away is the home of artists Bim and Arthur Giardelli. Now in his nineties, Arthur Giardelli was part of an intellectual circle of artists and poets that included David Jones, Ceri Richards and R S Thomas. He and his wife Bim moved to Wales during the Second World War, found Pembrokeshire and now live in a converted schoolhouse, The Golden Plover Art Gallery, where they exhibit their own paintings and those of artists they have collected over the years. The Giardellis are just two out of dozens of painters and creative artists

– people as diverse as J M W Turner and Graham Sutherland – who have found something magical in the Pembrokeshire landscape and light.

And so on to Freshwater West. There is no finer view in the whole of Wales than when you crest the hill to the south-east of the bay and gain your first glimpse of those wide, golden sands. On a rough day, when the tide is full, breakers hurl themselves at the beach in a fury of swirling white foam. Then the surfers are out in force, sweeping in on the crests of the waves like demented acrobats on their boards.

Take time to gaze back towards flat-topped Linney Head, limestone which was lifted up above sea level about 80 million years ago. The headland, like much of the ground to the east, is inaccessible because of the MOD firing ranges. However, it is now possible to take part in guided walks from Linney Head to Stack Rocks several times each year, walks which are arranged and conducted by the National Park Authority as part of their activities and events programme.

The GREEN BRIDGE OF WALES – on a quiet, calm day

Rugged and open to the elements, FRESHWATER WEST sands are one of the most famous of all Pembrokeshire beaches

PEN-Y-HOLT stack off the south Pembrokeshire coast

20

Dozens of tiny streams run down across the beach and dunes at Freshwater West, the water cutting deeply into the soft bed of Old Red Sandstone. Many of the bays, particularly to the north, are inaccessible and the sands themselves are plagued by dangerous quicksand and a strong under-tow which has claimed the lives of many swimmers over the years.

The beach was, in the past, renowned for its laver bread, a traditional Welsh delicacy. The edible seaweed (porphyra umbilicalis, to give it the correct name) from which laver bread is made flourished here. The dunes used to be home to around 20 small huts where the seaweed was dried and then stored before being mashed and cooked. Now only one hut remains, having recently been refurbished by the Friends of the National Park.

The sand dunes at Freshwater West are relatively low lying and have been designated a Site of Special Scientific Interest. Here you will find unusual plants like sea rocket and prickly saltwort and, of course, the long-rooted marram grass which is able to reach down deeply into the earth to find water. The dunes are also full of adders, beautifully marked but decidedly poisonous. The snakes are timid, however, and will rarely attack unless threatened or provoked.

Freshwater West has been a graveyard for many fine ships, caught on the lee shore when beating in for safety with a fierce westerly gale behind them. At very low tide you can still see the keel of one of these victims, possibly the Portuguese brig *Gram Para* which hit the sands in dense fog on 7th May 1855, spewing her cargo of india rubber and nuts along the coast and becoming a total wreck.

The seaweed hut at FRESHWATER WEST

One of the many wrecks that litter the Pembrokeshire coast – this one is on FRESHWATER WEST beach

The most famous disaster on the beach, however, occurred in 1943 when LCGs (Landing Craft, Guns) 15 and 16 sank just a few hundred yards offshore. Bound for Falmouth the unwieldy craft ran into heavy weather in Cardigan Bay but, for some unaccountable reason, they were refused permission to shelter either in Fishguard or Milford Haven. The vessels ploughed on and were eventually over-whelmed by mountainous seas just off Freshwater West beach. LCG 15 sank within sight and hearing of the helpless watchers on the sands, hundreds of young Royal Marines on board being drowned in the pounding seas. LCG 16 foundered a few hours later.

The tragedy wasn't over. A naval sloop, HMS *Rosemary*, was one of several vessels to attempt a rescue. She was unable to get a line across to the stricken LCG 16 and six sailors volunteered to take it in one of the sloop's whalers. It, too, was swamped and the sailors drowned. In all, only three people survived from the two landing craft, the worst wartime disaster of its type in Britain. The affair was hurriedly hushed up by the authorities, only too well aware of their negligence in failing to allow the vessels to seek refuge in the calm waters of Milford Haven.

North-west of Freshwater West, beyond Broomhill Burrows, are East and West Pickard Bay. There is an Iron Age fort here, the remains of its single defensive bank clearly visible to the naked eye. Just inland lies RAF Angle air station. This Second World War airfield was just one of eight wartime aerodromes in Pembrokeshire and the only one of them to act as a fighter base. A large number of the pilots here were Czech, flying single-engine Spitfires or Hurricanes out over the sea, escorting vital convoys which had assembled in the Milford Haven waterway.

Angle was the scene of a dramatic crash landing in May 1943. A Sunderland of the Royal Australian Air Force, based at Pembroke Dock, was forced to put down on the airfield – the first time that such a huge flying boat had ever landed on grass rather than water. When the war ended, RAF Angle's useful life was over but traces of the place can still be found if you are prepared to brave the wind and elements on this rugged cliff top.

Sheep Island sits at the western end of the headland, a low-lying and gnarled fist of rock which, at first sight, appears to be still connected to the mainland. The remnants of an Iron Age fort, dating from about 300 BC, can still be seen on its grassy slopes, despite the attempts of the Admiralty to destroy it when they constructed a U boat lookout base across the walls of the fort during the First World War. The island remains inhospitable and unwelcoming.

A typical deserted cove, one of many to be found in PEMBROKESHIRE

Beyond Sheep Island lies the equally unprepossessing Rat Island. The name alone is enough to discourage visitors! East Blockhouse overlooks Rat Island. The Armada threat of 1588 inspired the idea of a watchtower and fort on this site but it was modified and re-designed during the Napoleonic invasion scare of the early 1800s. More up-to-date gun emplacements were added in 1900 – part of the defence plan for nearby Pembroke Dockyard – and even more modifications came during the Second World War when an anti-aircraft battery was added. If you care to search diligently, you can still find elements of each stage in the fort's development.

The village of Angle is at the tip of a small peninsula which marks the southern arm of Milford Haven. It is a single-street community, houses lining the road connecting West Angle Bay and Angle Bay proper (East Angle Bay as it is known locally). East Angle Bay is a muddy tidal backwater, not without a certain grace and charm, but the sands of West Angle are gently sloping and protected from the elements by twin headlands on either side of the bay. It is ideal for swimming and boating.

Just off shore lies Thorn Island, one of several defensive forts built in the middle of the nineteenth century to protect the dockyard at nearby Pembroke Dock. The island itself is only a few acres in size and the old Victorian fort covers virtually all of its flat surface. This was one of the famous Palmerston follies, fortresses which were built around the coast of Britain whilst Lord Palmerston was foreign secretary. In the middle years of Victoria's reign, war with France seemed a distinct possibility and Palmerston applied to Parliament for money to build a series of forts to protect the coast. By the time the money was approved the threat from France had vanished but the forts were duly built, nevertheless. Hence the derogatory name.

Thorn Island fort was begun in 1852 and finished in 1859, at a cost of £85,000. Designed to house nine heavy calibre guns and 100 artillerymen, the fort never fired a shot in anger and was soon abandoned. It has since been used as a hotel and, indeed, there are plans in hand for it to be re-designed for the same purpose in the future – complete with cable car access from the mainland. The island is most famous, however, as the site of a genuine Welsh 'Whiskey Galore'.

Bound for Adelaide with a cargo of 7,500 cases of 100 per-cent-proof whiskey, the *Loch Shiel* went ashore on the rocks of Thorn Island on the night of 30th January 1894. As if the whiskey wasn't enough, the ship was also carrying 7,000 cases of beer and a large quantity of dynamite – a dangerous and lethal mixture. A heavy sea was running and it quickly became apparent that the ship's pumps could not keep out the water. A mattress soaked in paraffin was lit on the deck as a distress signal and the Angle lifeboat, in a courageous and exemplary rescue, took off the passengers and crew.

The real story of the *Loch Shiel*, however, was only just beginning. As the ship started to break up, her cargo floated ashore and, despite prompt attendance of Customs officials, much of it was immediately spirited away by hundreds of locals who soon appeared on the beach. The whiskey and beer were hidden in gardens, behind swiftly boarded-over alcoves and in attics. Bottles of whiskey were even concealed down the legs of women's bloomers in order to get them past the eagled-eyed Customs men!

There is a tragic side to the story. Three men died; a father and son drowned while trying to pull a crate from the water and another man perished from alcohol poisoning and exposure after lying drunk in a hedge all night. The death toll could have been higher, several locals gleefully carrying home their treasure only to discover that what they had purloined was not whiskey or beer but gunpowder!

Bottles of *Loch Shiel* whiskey, long forgotten and ignored, are still occasionally found in Angle houses which are being renovated or restored. In October 1999 members of the Adventurous Divers Club discovered half a dozen bottles of the ship's beer on the seabed near Thorn Island – beer which was then well over a hundred years old.

Angle village is a pretty place, well worth meandering through. Field boundaries on each side of the single main street show the remains of medieval field systems and many of the houses are, themselves, traditional workers' cottages. Devil's Quoit, a burial chamber dating from 3000 BC, can be found a mile or so out of the village, just off the main road to Pembroke. This superb example of a prehistoric menhir is just one of hundreds of ancient remains scattered across the county. A good Ordnance Survey map will show you exactly where these monuments lie. Superbly atmospheric, they are well worth a visit by anyone who has even the faintest sense of history and interest in our past.

The pride of Angle is the Tower House (also known locally as the Old Rectory or Peele Tower) which dates from the fourteenth century. Its origins remain unclear. It was probably the house of the Sherbourne family, the first lords of Angle but this has never been confirmed. It remains a superb example of a fortified house from the medieval period.

The tower is now all that is left of a much larger building which would originally have had both a walled enclosure and a moat – entrance to the tower could only be achieved via a doorway on the first floor. This would have been reached by using a wooden drawbridge. The Tower House was restored by the National Park Authority several years ago and is now Wales' only surviving tower house, although there are dozens of examples to be found in Scotland, Ireland and the northern counties of England.

In the seventeenth century Angle was a famous sanctuary for pirates and smugglers who haunted the Welsh coast. The notorious John Callice operated out of the village inn here, a place owned by the local Customs officer at Pembroke – thus confirming Dr Johnson's opinion that if there was one thing worse than a smuggler, it was the revenue man who was supposed to catch him!

These days Angle is a quiet backwater. Even at the height of the summer season holidaymakers don't dominate the place to the extent that they do in Saundersfoot or Tenby. It remains a peaceful village with two vastly different but equally interesting bays where the visitor or casual interloper can sit, relax and watch the world pass happily by.

THORN ISLAND

The Tower House at ANGLE, dating from the fourteenth century

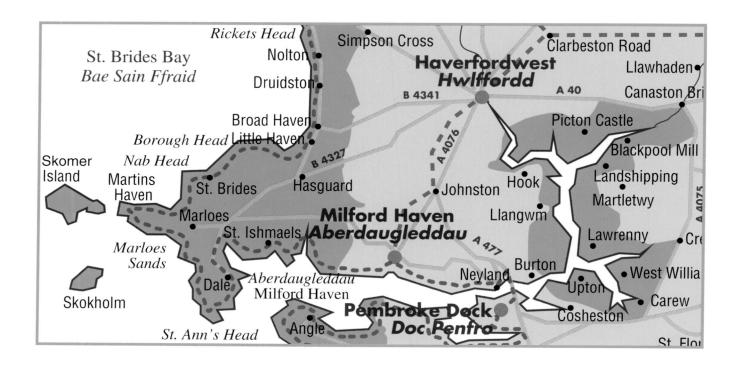

Chapter Three: The Milford Haven Waterway

WHEN you think of the Pembrokeshire coast your mind immediately turns to soaring sea cliffs and long golden beaches. You rarely consider the Milford Haven waterway even though it is, in reality, as much a part of the coast as Freshwater West or Strumble Head or Poppit Sands.

The Haven is a wide, immensely deep estuary which is flanked by low hills for much of its length. Once a river valley, it was flooded when water levels – which were precisely some 130 feet lower than today – began to rise at the end of the Ice Age. This was between 5,000 and 10,000 years ago, when sea water made its way gradually into the valley which had been carved out along a fault line. The result is the Haven as we know it today.

At a vaguely indefinable point towards its eastern extremity, just above the village of Burton on its northern shore, the Haven transforms itself into the Cleddau River. Further upstream the river itself splits into two, one branch heading towards Haverfordwest and the Preseli Mountains, the other snaking up past Canaston Bridge and Llawhaden, towards the Llys-y-frân Country Park. The Milford Haven waterway and Cleddau River dominate the map of Pembrokeshire, splitting it into two at a point somewhat south of centre. Since the influence of man was first felt in this area, the Haven has been in constant use as a waterway and means of communication.

The Bluestones of Stonehenge, for example, came from the Preseli Mountains to the north. Highly desirable as a material with which to make axes, the Bluestones (or, more accurately, the spotted dolerites) were viewed as sacred by the people who built Stonehenge. Around that time it is more than likely that a large number of stones were dragged to the headwaters of the Cleddau, floated down into the estuary itself and out into the open sea. It would have been a hazardous operation, taking many years to complete and, in all probability, seeing a large number of the precious stones falling to a final resting place on the bottom of the Haven. However long it took, the Milford Haven waterway would probably have been a means of transporting the stones to Wiltshire where they were positioned to make up the inner horseshoe of the Stonehenge circle.

Oil jetties in MILFORD HAVEN

Milford Haven is blessed with dozens of tidal creeks along its shores and these support a wealth of bird and marine life. The area is an important habitat both for migrating species and for those birds which are resident in the county all year long. Here you will find, amongst others, ringed plover, redshank, oystercatchers, grebe, cormorants and grey herons. However, this is also the most densely populated part of the county and it is the history of the Haven that really forces itself upon the visitors' imagination.

Shakespeare knew about Milford Haven, of course, and in *Cymbeline* (Act III, Scene ii) wrote

> Tell me how Wales was made so happy as
> To inherit such a haven.

He called the waterway 'blessed' – a sentiment echoed by people as diverse as Daniel Defoe in his *A Tour Through the Whole Island of Great Britain* and Admiral Horatio Nelson. Although the famous admiral was not the regular visitor that popular legend declares, he was clear that Milford Haven provided the finest spot in the whole country for the assembly of a British fleet. The estuary, he said, even rivalled Trincomalee in Sri Lanka (formerly known as Ceylon) as one of the most wonderful harbours he had ever seen.

The Haven's greatest assets are its deep water and its sheltered shores. The raiding Norsemen of the Dark Ages certainly seem to have appreciated this fact. They attacked the Pembrokeshire coast many times between the eighth and eleventh centuries, burning St Davids Cathedral on at least eight separate occasions and often using Milford Haven as a temporary base.

Over time the Norsemen grew weary of constant war and raiding and began to settle in the places which they had once burned. Pembrokeshire was no different from any other coastal area. In 837, for example, Viking chieftain Hubba wintered in the Haven, reputedly with 23 longships. He probably gave his name to Hubberston at the mouth of the estuary and, even more certainly, he and his warriors increased the local birth rate by many hundredfold.

Other Pembrokeshire place names, apart from Hubberston, have Viking origins – Herbrandston, Freystrop, Skokholm and Skomer Islands to name just a few. Even Carr Rocks, off the town of Pembroke Dock, take their name from the Norse word 'skare' which actually means 'rocks'.

There is a school of thought amongst historians that central government in London largely ignored Milford Haven in that long interregnum between the Viking raids and the Napoleonic Wars. This is not strictly true.

When Arnulph, son of the earl of Montgomery, came to Pembroke in 1093 he was probably engaged on a commando raid, reconnoitring the area ahead of a full-scale assault by his father's troops. He would have sailed up the Haven – the easiest and most logical way to travel – until he sighted the rocky headland on which he soon built his stronghold. Fifty or so years later, the famous Richard Strongbow launched his conquest of Ireland from the castle at Pembroke and the wide waters of Milford Haven.

In 1171 King Henry II gathered his own invasion force in the estuary, prior to an attack on Ireland. On that recorded occasion he assembled a fleet of over 400 warships, the largest armada ever to come together in the waterway. In the summer of 1485 Henry Tudor landed on the north shore of the Haven to begin his glorious march to Bosworth Field and the throne of England. Royalists and Parliamentarians thought the estuary so significant and such a tactical lynch pin that, during the English Civil War, they both stationed battle fleets there.

Clearly, then, Milford Haven was not entirely forgotten. The trouble was, British governments were never proactive in their military policies. Events had to virtually overwhelm them before they would react and it was only the French landings at Fishguard in 1797 that made the government of William Pitt realise the nation's best defence lay in a strong and vigilant navy. A strong navy meant the creation of dockyards to build warships. As far as the Haven was concerned such yards were established, first at Milford, and later at Pembroke Dock. Dockyards have to be defended and the nineteenth century saw a proliferation of forts and gun emplacements springing up along the Haven. The modern-day visitor can see several of these forts which still stand as a silent tribute to engineers and military planners from a long-gone age when enemies were obvious and alliances a matter of honour.

If the nineteenth century brought the military and navy to the waterway, the twentieth brought oil. These days, if you take a boat up the Haven or a car along its flanks, it is the oil refineries and jetties which will stay in your memory. They mar the foreshore and the flanking hills but, in a strange and indefinable way, are not without a certain interest and charm.

Conscious of the wide waters and deep channels of the area BP built the first oil refinery and tanker terminal opposite the town of Milford Haven in 1957 at Popton Fort. It was linked by pipeline to their refinery in Llandarcy. Three years later they were followed by Esso who built their refinery outside the

Paradox – the MILFORD HAVEN oil refineries at night, a light show worthy of Disneyland

town, across the river from BP. Regent Oil Company (the name later being changed to Texaco) arrived in 1964, followed by Gulf in 1968 and Amoco in 1973. The deep waters of the Haven meant that huge super-tankers of over 200,000 tons could be easily accommodated at any stage of the tide.

The worldwide oil industry suffered a severe recession during the 1980s and several of the Haven refineries either closed or changed hands. The jetties remain, however, dominating the waterway – so much so that it is now impossible to gaze at that six-mile sweep of water and imagine the estuary without the all-pervading quays, walkways and gantries.

From the village of Angle the road takes you eastwards along the flank of the Haven. Take time, however, to visit the wide expanse of Angle Bay. If the tide is out, there is a superb two-mile walk along the foreshore. It will certainly repay the effort. Quite apart from a wide range of waders and duck, you will also come across the rotting timbers of the *Progress*, one of the many vessels which, in the nineteenth century, ran cod from Newfoundland to Milford Haven. The remains of the *Mary Jane*, the last ship to be built at the private dockyard of Jacobs Pill on Pembroke River, can also be found in this mud-encrusted bay.

The dead village of Rhoscrowther sits at the eastern end of Angle Bay, dwarfed by the menacing shadows of the Texaco oil refinery. Over the years there have been a number of serious explosions at Texaco and on at least two separate occasions the residents of Rhoscrowther were forced to flee for their lives. After an enormous explosion in the catalytic cracker of the plant in January 1992 many villagers felt too frightened to return to their homes.

Consequently, Texaco bought each house in the village, an exercise which cost the company over £2 million, and the villagers moved elsewhere.

Disaster and the oil industry often seem to go hand in hand. Whilst the refineries undoubtedly brought jobs and a degree of wealth to the Haven, events like the *Sea Empress* wreck of 1996 showed how dangerous a tightrope the county was walking with regards to the oil industry.

The *Sea Empress* went ashore on the rocks just off St Ann's Head on the night of 15th February, spewing 72,000 tons of oil into the waters of the Haven. It was the third-worst oil spill in British maritime history, thousands of sea birds and fish dying in the disaster. A six-week clean-up operation salvaged what could have been an ecological holocaust but at a cost of somewhere in the region of £60 million! The balance between industry and tourism has always been a delicate one and although, by and large, it is a balance which Pembrokeshire has been able to maintain – thanks in no small part to the efforts of the Pembrokeshire National Park Authority – the danger of further ecological misfortune has not yet been removed.

The BP pumping station, which used to lie to the east of Angle Bay, closed in 1985, the company leasing its jetties to nearby Texaco and leaving the Victorian remains of Popton Fort to the Field Studies Council Research Centre. Popton Fort is yet another of the many military establishments sited along the Haven. The forts on this waterway are unusual in that nearly all of them date from the same period, eleven out of the fourteen being built within a 'window' of just twenty years. Whilst their primary purpose was defence against attack from the sea, nearly all of them also had substantial barracks accommodation, thus making them able to resist assault from the landward side as well. No invaders ever came, however, and so the forts and their defences were never put to the test.

Pembroke River is a tributary of the Haven, a muddy backwater which snakes eastwards from Pennar Gut. Don't let the mud and silt deceive you; a treacherous current still races down the centre of the stream and many unwary swimmers have lost their lives in this deceptive stretch of water.

The tiny village of Bentlass on the south shore of the river was the scene of one such tragedy in February 1889. It was usual practice for the women of the area to cross the stream each Friday, using a ferryboat run out of Bentlass by Mr Jones. They would go to the dockyard gates in Pembroke Dock, collect their husbands' pay packets and then shop in the market before returning to their homes in Monkton, Castlemartin, Hundleton and other villages around Pembroke. On the fateful day the river was in a wild state and, returning from the north shore, one of the women passengers panicked when water came in over the side of the small boat. She leaped to her feet, the boat lurched into the waves and was quickly overwhelmed by the tide. Jones the Boatman, a young boy who helped him run the ferry and all seven women passengers were drowned before help could reach them.

At Cat's Hole Cave on the banks of the river, barely a mile from the town of Pembroke, several important archaeological discoveries have been made. For thousands of years man used this cave, paddling up and down the river, slipping silently through the dense woods and forests along its shore. The cave was also almost certainly used by a Bronze Age carpenter and may even have been in use up to Norman times.

A fine series of flints, now in the National Museum of Wales, was discovered in the cave which stretches back for over a hundred feet into the limestone rock. When excavated in 1908 the cave was found to contain deposits up to a thickness of 4 feet. The place also yielded a bronze saw, chisel, a skull and animal remains which included hyena and mammoth.

Pembroke sits on a spur or promontory of land, in effect the western end of a long narrow limestone ridge. Approximately 1000 yards in length and just 200 yards wide, the ridge is flanked on the north and south by two narrow valleys which were once tidal inlets. The extreme western end of the ridge gathers itself into a rocky headland, not unlike a clenched fist at the end of a sinewy arm. Here, in 1093, the invading Normans built what the writer Giraldus Cambrensis once called 'a slender fortress of stakes and turf' and changed the character of the area for ever.

The town of PEMBROKE at the beginning of the twentieth century – apart from the traffic, little has changed

Mighty PEMBROKE CASTLE stands supreme

Pembroke Castle is the most impressive Norman fortress in the county. It was the seat of the earls of Pembroke, its crowning glory being the Great Keep which was built by Earl William Marshall in or around the year 1200. A far cry from the original motte-and-bailey of Arnulph de Montgomery, this tower is one of the finest examples of a round keep in Britain. The scene of much strife over the years, Pembroke Castle never fell to the Welsh and was the birthplace of Henry Tudor (later Henry VII) in 1456.

The town of Pembroke consists, largely, of a single street, running along the top of the ridge, and is a wonderfully atmospheric little place, full of interesting shops, buildings and by-ways. Parts of the original town walls still remain – surprising when you consider that Oliver Cromwell once appeared outside them and did his level best to batter the walls and town to dust.

The siege of Pembroke took place in 1648 and was part of the Second Civil War, that strange, unnecessary conflict when, with Charles I defeated and captured, many of the Parliamentarians changed sides and suddenly declared for the king. The defenders of Pembroke – Colonel Roland Laugharne and John Poyer, the town mayor – withstood Cromwell's battering for six long weeks. The walls of the castle and town were never breached and surrender only came when supplies ran low and it became clear that promised support from other Royalist forces was never going to materialise.

Local legend will tell you that a traitor revealed the location of the castle's water supply to Cromwell. With the water cut off, says the tale, Poyer and Laugharne had no option but to surrender. The traitor was then supposedly hung by Cromwell as a reward for his services. It is an interesting story but it has not even a grain of truth about it.

Laugharne and Poyer, together with Colonel Rice Powell from the Tenby garrison, were arraigned for treason and duly condemned to death. The Council of State decided on leniency, however, and said that only one of the three would have to die. Three pieces of paper were prepared, two bearing the legend 'Life Given by God', the other being blank – a decidedly strange way of deciding a man's fate, particularly by Puritans who despised all forms of gambling. Poyer drew the blank and was executed by firing squad on 25th April 1649.

It may seem unlikely to modern visitors but Pembroke was once a major port. In 1724 Daniel Defoe visited and in *A Tour Through the Whole Island of Great Britain* declared

> This is the largest and richest and most flourishing town of all South Wales ... near 200 sail ships belong to the town, small and great. In a word, all this part of Wales is a rich and flourishing country.

Products like wool, meat, grain and herring were regularly sent to north Wales and to countries as far away as Spain and Portugal. As coal mining in Pembrokeshire developed in the eighteenth century, so the quay at Pembroke seized its chance for a share in the new business. Small wonder, then, that Defoe found such a flourishing community – as the fine Georgian and Victorian houses along Main Street will testify.

Two miles to the north, over a steep ridge, lies the modern town of Pembroke Dock. In every respect, this is a classic example of a nineteenth-century 'new town'. The place did not exist until 1814 when the Admiralty decided to transfer its dockyard from nearby Milford Haven to a flat expanse of sheltered land lying in the lee of a steep ridge – an area then known as Paterchurch. The government already owned land in the area and, with lots of deep water close inshore, this was the ideal place to build ships.

The first two vessels, the 28-gunned *Valorous* and *Ariadne*, slid into the waters of the Haven in 1816 and Pembroke Dock's 112-year history of ship-building had begun. Over 260 ships were constructed here, ranging from *The Duke of Wellington* – the largest woodenwall ever to be built – to hundreds of tiny gunboats, from massive dreadnoughts like the *Hannibal* and *Repulse* to five Royal Yachts.

Like all dockyard towns, Pembroke Dock is full of interesting stories and legends but none of them is more bizarre than that of Betty Foggy and *HMS Caesar*. Due for launching on 21st June 1853, the whole population of the town came to witness the event including Betty Foggy who was popularly

supposed to be a witch. When she was refused entry to the yards, Betty cursed the ship, saying, 'There will be no launching today'. When the time came for the launch, the *Caesar* refused to move.

Actually it had nothing to do with Betty's curse. The Admiralty, ever conscious of finances, had ordered cheap but soft fir wood for the launching ways instead of the usual oak. As the *Caesar* was built she simply became heavier and heavier, bedding herself into the wood. The Admiralty conveniently seized on Betty's words, using them as an excuse for their own incompetence. Over the next two weeks they built huge camels, large wooden structures, beneath the ship in order to raise her out of the wood and then, when the town was conveniently at chapel or church one Sunday morning, the *Caesar* was launched. The Admiralty simply said, 'Betty has lifted her curse'.

When the dockyard closed in 1926 the town was left without purpose. An RAF flying-boat base was created in the old yards in 1930 and for many years the graceful Sunderlands of PD (as the base was popularly known) were a familiar sight on the waters of the Haven. It was only a brief respite, however, and when the RAF pulled out in the 1950s the town that was created to build ships was left, once more, without reason for existence.

Once the most advanced shipbuilding yard in the world, employing almost 4,000 men, the remains of the old dockyard can still be seen and enjoyed. The huge dockyard wall and two superb 'Martello' towers – one of which is now the Pembroke Dock

The Royal Naval dockyard at PEMBROKE DOCK in 1906 – the huge building sheds dominate the yards

The launch of the *James Watt* at PEMBROKE DOCK in April 1853 – from *The Illustrated London News*

Museum – give a good indication of how the place would have looked in its heyday.

The dockyard itself is still home for some local industry. Perhaps more importantly, it is now also a terminal for the Irish ferry service, boats regularly leaving from here for Rosslare. Lorries and cars trundle easily past the old dockyard gates, their occupants caring little about the importance of the place through which they are passing. And perhaps that's as it should be.

Pembroke Dock remains the largest urban community in Pembrokeshire. It is also the only truly industrial town in the whole county – Haverfordwest has always been a market town and while Milford and Neyland might have aspirations, they do not even come close to Pembroke Dock, a place spawned by industry and, ultimately, killed by it as well. The streets of the town are wide and gracious, partly with designs of grandeur but mainly to enable easy transportation of raw materials which, in the days before the railway arrived, had to come into the yards by road.

The remains of Jacob's Pill dockyard lie over the ridge to the south of the town, close to the suburb

of Pennar. This was one of many small shipbuilding concerns around the Haven and was the brainchild of Edward Reed, one time chief constructor at the Admiralty. In June 1877 the armoured corvette *Hi Yei* was launched from the yards, one of the first armoured warships in the Imperial Japanese Navy – an early example of Anglo-Japanese co-operation. All that now remains of Jacob's Pill are two long depressions in the grass, a few walls and the ruins of the old mould loft.

Known now as the Cleddau River, the Haven waterway flows on beyond Pembroke Dock. This is the Daugleddau, the region of the two Cleddau rivers, and here thick woodland often runs down to the water's edge. These woods are home to a wide range of wildlife like badgers, rabbits and foxes. Dozens of tiny villages, places such as Llangwm, Lawrenny, Burton, Cresswell Quay and Cosheston, are situated on the banks of the river and its tributaries. Many of them once boasted small ship-building yards or ferries and in several places the diligent visitor will be able to spot the rotting remains of wooden barges which used to ply their trade on this stretch of river.

CAREW CASTLE, scene of the last great tournament in Britain

CAREW CASTLE gazes on its own reflection

Several places along this quiet river were once renowned for being part of the Pembrokeshire coalfield, in particular the small community of Hook. At Landshipping, in 1845, the first national mining disaster occurred when the river suddenly and unexpectedly burst into Garden Pit and drowned more than forty miners – some of them young boys.

Carew Castle sits at the head of the Carew River, a small tidal creek just off the Cleddau. The castle is a hybrid – pure Norman on its southern walls, Elizabethan mansion on the north. The last great tournament held in Britain took place here in 1507, organised by the castle's owner, Sir Rhys ap Thomas, to celebrate his award of the Order of the Garter. Lasting for five days, the tournament was attended by noblemen from all over Wales and consisted of combats such as jousting and wrestling. Theatricals, poetry readings and musical events also took place.

If you pause to look at Carew Castle, make sure that you also take time to view the nearby 14-foot-high Celtic Cross which was carved in the eleventh century to commemorate Mereddud ap Edwin of Deheubarth. There is also a fine tidal mill here and the village is beautifully calm and relaxing.

Heading back towards the sea, you cross the river by the Cleddau Bridge, high above Pembroke Ferry. This modern structure replaced the old car ferry in 1975 but not before a dramatic collapse took place on the Pembroke Dock side in June 1970. A section of the box girder construction was being cantilevered into position when it fell, killing several workmen and putting back completion of the bridge by two or three years. The bridge is undoubtedly efficient, and the views off the top are spectacular, but it doesn't have even half of the atmosphere of the old ferryboat.

The Celtic Cross at CAREW

The CLEDDAU BRIDGE spans the Milford Haven waterway

The town of Neyland, just opposite Pembroke Dock, is now home to a busy marina which nestles into a tributary stream, virtually underneath the Cleddau Bridge. Originally called New Milford, Neyland was the site selected by Isambard Kingdom Brunel as the western terminus for the South Wales Railway. Prosperity loomed as, in the wake of the railway, the town became a terminal for the Irish packet service. Unfortunately, in 1906 this service was transferred to Fishguard and Neyland began to decline in importance. The place had its small fishing fleet for a while and the railway yards lasted until the 1960s but, really, once the ferry service left, Neyland's dreams of glory were over.

There had been shipbuilding along the north shore of the Haven for many years, particularly at Hazelbeach and Neyland itself and in the winter of 1860-61 the famous *Great Eastern* lay here for several months, the name now commemorated in the town's Great Eastern Terrace. Thousands of visitors came to view the largest ship in the world, the liner

grandeur. He drew up plans for the town, for quays, for a dockyard and a market and put the whole project into the hands of his nephew, Charles Greville. It was Greville who introduced Sir William to Emma Hart, soon to become his second wife and, in due course, the mistress of Lord Nelson. Sir William was over sixty when they married, Emma just twenty-six. For several years the Hamiltons and Nelson lived together in a bizarre ménage à trois. It must have been the worst-kept secret in the world; the only people who thought the secret was safe being Sir William, Emma and Nelson. The Lord Nelson Hotel in Milford Haven still marks the place where Nelson and Emma stayed during a visit to the area in 1802.

The new town grew quickly, thanks in no small part to the efforts of a group of Quakers, whalers from Nantucket. Greville offered them a new life in the town after their loyalty to the English crown during the War of Independence led to persecution by the new American state. The whaling trade did not survive for long but Milford Haven soon

The docks and fishing boats at MILFORD shown in the early years of the twentieth century

lying on a specially constructed grid of iron and steel, dwarfing the houses behind her and dominating the river in front.

Sir William Hamilton founded the town of Milford Haven in 1790. A rich Scot, he was left the land where the modern town now stands when his first wife died. Sir William certainly had dreams of

developed a fishing fleet which eventually grew to such an extent that the place became the third-largest fishing port in Britain. A popular local tale declares that, at one time, the port was so full of trawlers that you could walk from one side of the docks to the other over their decks and thus save yourself the halfpenny fee on the town's toll bridge.

Stack Rock Fort in MILFORD HAVEN

(photo: Mike Edwards)

Although the industry declined greatly in the 1960s there is still a fishing fleet of sorts in Milford docks.

Sir William Hamilton's dockyard was established in the town at the beginning of the nineteenth century but by 1814 it had moved up river to Pembroke Dock, leaving Milford Haven to contemplate what might have been. It was not until the 1870s that Milford docks were finally completed, opening for business in 1888. By then it was far too late to secure any sort of foothold in the transatlantic trade, most of this having been firmly and irrevocably captured by Liverpool. The large liners that the planners and dreamers had hoped would one day come to the Haven never really materialised.

Just off Milford lies the strange circular shape of Stack Rock fort, yet another of the Palmerston follies built to protect the yards at Pembroke Dock. The fort is perfectly preserved, mainly because it is so isolated and unapproachable out in the Haven. There are several other forts around this area, places like Hubberston, South Hook and Dale Point Battery, all of them designed to give covering fire and to link with the emplacements on the other side of the Haven.

ST ANN'S HEAD seen from the air

Just before the village of Dale you will find the Gann. This strangely named but striking ridge of shingle is the edge of a deposit of sand and gravel which was thrown up when the Irish Sea ice sheet melted some 18,000 years ago. During the Second World War much of the shingle was taken away and used as hard core on the emergency wartime airfields of Talbenny and Dale. As a consequence, there are now deep pits in the gravel and these have since been flooded by the sea. They provide an important habitat for wading birds and for wildfowl like snipe which use the area as a winter home.

Dale has a long seafaring tradition, being renowned as a smuggling village in the late fifteenth century. Situated at the mouth of the Haven, just to the north-west of St Ann's Head, the village was an ideal spot for coastal traders to drop off their goods and a regular business gradually grew up with ports along the Bristol Channel. Dale is famous as being the sunniest place in Wales, the peninsula having some of the lowest rainfall figures in the country. Partly as a consequence of this, the village and beach have now become a popular water sports centre.

To the south of Dale lies Mill Bay. Here on 7th August 1485 Henry Tudor landed with a mercenary force of about 2,000 French soldiers, intending to make one last attempt to seize the throne of England. Opposing him was Sir Rhys ap Thomas, who held these lands in wild west Wales for King Richard III.

There is a lovely story about Rhys and Henry on that fateful August day, one which has gone down in the folklore of this part of the country. It seems that Rhys had given King Richard his word of honour to protect the west. 'Henry shall only enter this land over my body,' he supposedly declared. When Henry landed at Mill Bay, the two men walked to nearby Mullock Bridge where Rhys lay beneath the planks. Henry strolled over the bridge, over the body of Rhys in fact, thus ensuring that the Welshman did not break his word. It is a wonderful tale which might, just, have a grain of truth about it.

St Ann's Head marks the limit of Milford Haven on this northern shore. You can visit the lighthouse and the coastguard base, created in 1966 on the site of the original lighthouse – which was, in turn, built over a chapel established by Henry Tudor. The first light on the headland, an area often swept by gales, was erected in 1713. Passing ships would pay a toll of one penny per ton of cargo (two pennies if they were a foreign vessel) in order to fund the warning light. The modern lighthouse is fully automatic and is visible from 20 miles away.

The scenery here at the furthest extremity of the Haven is spectacular. You feel as if you are standing on the edge of the world and when you gaze out towards Angle peninsula on the other side of the waterway the view would be very similar to that glimpsed by Henry Tudor in 1485.

This stretch of water is commonly known as the Heads. Beyond lies the Atlantic and America. On a wild day, when waves pound onto the rocks of St Ann's Head, you can truly understand the emotion when people mutter, 'God help sailors on a day like this.'

The lighthouse on St Ann's Head

opposite: Calm waters of the Western Cleddau
(photo: John Fenna)

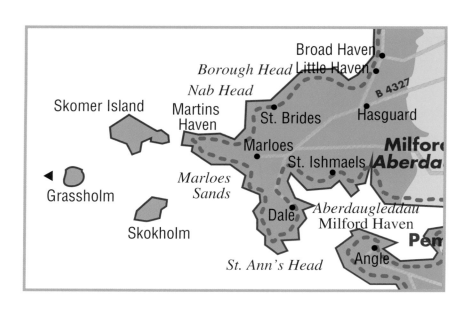

Chapter Four

Dale to Broad Haven

ESPITE the fact that Dale village is supposedly one of the sunniest places in Wales, the Dale Peninsula is invariably swept by severe gales during the autumn and winter months. These give the area a decidedly 'wind-blown' appearance. It's hardly surprising as the south-facing peninsula is relatively flat and when storms and winds whip in off the sea, they do so with a ferocity and a sharpness which are like a million knives lancing into your unprotected body.

Marloes Sands dominates this stretch of coast. The beach is long and curving, a magnificent area of golden sands which is rivalled only by Freshwater West across the Haven. The cliffs behind Marloes beach are a magnet for geologists who come to study the exposed sections of sedimentary rocks formed during the Silurian period approximately 400 million years ago.

The Three Chimneys formation in the centre of the bay is a nearly vertical section, made up of alternating layers of sandstone and mudstone. This dramatic and famous spectacle was caused by the collision of continents some 290 million years ago and while the soft mudstone has gradually been eroded by the weather, the harder sandstone layers still protrude – very much like flying buttresses on medieval cathedrals or churches.

In a memorable gale of November 1954 a fourth chimney was actually snapped off, leaving behind just the Three Chimneys that we see today. During the same storm the anemometer at nearby HMS Harrier, a Naval Air Direction Centre, registered a gust of 130 mph and actually went off the scale. Local people will gleefully tell you the story of the base chaplain who, during the gale, was lying awake in bed, wondering if the roof of his hut would survive the winds. At that moment the whole hut promptly took off and disappeared into the night. Small wonder, then, that the base, which included a radar and meteorological school, was closed in 1960.

MARLOES

(photo: Philip Clarke)

The Three Chimneys at MARLOES

At the north end of Marloes Sands lies Gateholm Island, easily approached on foot when the tide is out, completely insular at other times of day. The point opposite Gateholm is known as the Horse's Neck and from here, if the light is right, it is possible to see the marks of ancient settlements on the flanks of the island. These early medieval remains may well have been a Christian settlement but archaeological finds have also included Roman coins and an ancient bronze pin.

Many of the Pembrokeshire Islands once housed religious communities or individual cells. Presumably the remoteness of the islands would have appealed to the early Christians and their desire for privacy. However, you cannot help wondering about the masochistic nature of these men, seeking refuge and solace on such windswept and desolate outcrops when a warm monastery or priory would, surely, have been a more logical alternative.

Gateholm is only one of many similar fists of rock dotted around the Pembrokeshire coast. Just off-shore from here lie Skomer Island and its adjacent Midland Isle. Skomer is reachable by boat from Martin's Haven in the summer months. These days the island is a nature reserve, run by the Wildlife Trust South and West Wales. It is famous for its puffins and Manx shearwaters, burrowing birds

GATEHOLM ISLAND, Marloes, reachable by foot at low tide

which have created a series of deep holes across the terrain. Visitors need to take care when walking on the island as it is all too easy to collapse this intricate network of tunnels which has been dug into the soil.

It's the very isolation of places like Skomer which has drawn the birds to make their homes here. Being burrowing creatures, making their nests in the earth, the puffins and shearwaters are easy prey to rats and foxes. The remote island terrain is perfect for them.

Skomer was farmed during the Iron Age and the remains of many old field enclosures and huts have been discovered here. After the coming of the

SKOMER ISLAND sits low and menacing in the water

Normans, the place was used to breed rabbits – something of a delicacy for the invaders – and was then largely abandoned until the middle of the eighteenth century when it was once more extensively farmed. This lasted until after the Second World War, the last farmer to force a living from the island's soil being Reuben Codd. A man of immense strength and ability, Codd went to become, literally, a legend in his own lifetime in the Pembrokeshire area.

The island is largely made up of Silurian volcanic lava, the rocks rising gently to a maximum height of 260 feet above sea level. Jack Sound separates Skomer from the mainland, a wild tide race which only the foolhardy or the very skilled should attempt to cross. The sea around Skomer has been designated a Marine Nature Reserve, the first of its kind in Britain. The Garland Stone, off the north cliffs of the island, is a favourite spot for basking grey seals while the bays and inlets facing Jack Sound provide superb territory for seals to have their pups each September and October.

Further out into the Atlantic lie Skokholm and Grassholm. Skokholm is renowned as the former home of R M Lockley, the naturalist who wrote a number of very popular books about the island, the birds he encountered and his life there. Run as a rabbit warren in the Middle Ages and farmed intensively in the nineteenth century, Skokholm was the scene of a dramatic birth in the years before the First World War. Jack 'Bulldog' Edwards was farming the island and a fierce storm prevented his wife crossing to Martin's Haven for her confinement. The baby was born on Skokholm but it is not really surprising that the family left the island shortly afterwards.

Although Bulldog Edwards finished farming the island in 1912, R M Lockley came to Skokholm in 1927 and lived there until the outbreak of the Second World War. His studies of the seabirds on the island effectively created a Bird Observatory, the first of its kind in Britain, in 1933. You can still visit the place but only on certain days of the week. Together with Skomer and Grassholm it is renowned for its guillemots, Manx shearwaters and storm petrels. Between them, Skomer, Skokholm and the tiny Midland Isle have approximately 150,000 pairs of Manx shearwaters. It remains the world's largest breeding population of shearwaters.

You will find many other birds out on the islands – and, indeed, on the cliffs of the mainland as well. Cormorants and shags tend to live on the grassy cliff edges, the cormorants standing with their wings spread like giant scarecrows on the slopes overlooking

Puffins sit elegantly and wait on SKOMER

the sea – the only obvious way to distinguish them from shags. Hunting birds like peregrine falcons, kestrels and buzzards regularly hover above the cliffs, diving at small birds and other prey.

Grassholm is situated seven miles west of Skomer. Long renowned for its gannets – it is in fact the world's largest gannetry – the island's flanks are green with fescue, when they are not covered by the white feathers and droppings of the gannets or by other birds like kittiwakes and razorbills. The smell of guano is sometimes quite overpowering. In the *Mabinogion*, the famous stories and legends of Wales long ago, the island is known as Gwales and is the place where mighty Bendigeidfran's severed head is brought after he is killed in battle. Smaller than Skomer and Skokholm, the island of Grassholm has a charm which is hard to define and is all the more elusive because there is no public access or landing on Grassholm.

Gannets cover the flank of GRASSHOLM ISLAND

Twenty miles out into the Atlantic, beyond Grassholm Island, lie the Smalls. Constantly swept by waves, these rocks saw the creation of an early lighthouse, the famous Smalls Light, in 1776. Most visitors to Pembrokeshire will never get to see the Smalls but they remain as a rugged reminder of the potential cruelty of this coastline.

The Pembrokeshire Islands are an important part of the coastal experience. There are over a hundred

Basking seals on the PEMBROKESHIRE coast

islands off the coast of Wales and the Pembrokeshire examples are some of the most atmospheric of them all. They are uninhabited now (apart from Caldey) and are mostly designated as nature reserves. You need to take advice about visiting them as access is limited and restricted. National Park and Tourist Information Centres are probably the best places to start looking for help if you are planning to take a trip.

Back on the mainland, Albion Sands lie beyond the Horse's Neck and Gateholm Island, the beach being named after a paddle steamer called the *Albion* which went aground here on her maiden voyage in 1837. Fifty passengers managed to get safely ashore, together with the cargo of 180 pigs. The pigs soon disappeared into the houses and stock pens of local farmers and villagers – it was said that the smell of frying bacon hung around the houses of nearby Marloes for many long months!

The hedgerows in this area are, in season, full of flowers like violets, red campion, bluebells and primroses. Gorse also thrives here – invariably known as furzy in the south Pembrokeshire dialect.

This part of the coast is a bird-watchers' paradise. Shags and cormorants abound and the wide empty beaches are an ideal place to watch oystercatchers probing at the sand or mud with their long beaks. Increasingly rare yellowhammers, with their distinctive call, can be found here and choughs – rare in other areas of Britain – are actually thriving on this part of the coastline. A member of the crow and raven family, the choughs are often seen gathered together in large colonies, and are easily recognisable by their bright red legs and beaks.

Spend time on this stretch of coast and you will almost certainly spot grey seals. If you are lucky you might also see dolphins or porpoise. You need patience and time but, then, time should never be that important on the Pembrokeshire coast.

At Martin's Haven there is an exhibition about the marine life of the area but you should also pause to consider the famous Deer Park. The huge wall that marks the park was built by Lord Kensington, the local landowner, when he enclosed the area in 1847. At one stroke Kensington deprived many of the smallholders and tenant farmers around Marloes of their living, an event made even more poignant and pointless when you realise that the park probably never saw any deer and has now largely been returned to moorland.

The wall that marks the extent of the Deer Park is high and heavily buttressed. It must have cost Lord Kensington a fortune to build and may well have contributed to the family's financial problems at the end of the nineteenth century. A local story declares that, somewhere along the length of the wall, lies the body of a young girl. She was apparently thrown out of 'the big house' when it was discovered that she had been having an affair with the mason in charge of building the wall.

Musselwick Sands is another fine stretch of beach but it is only really accessible at low tide. Visitors need to take care as it is all too easy to be cut off by the advancing sea. Marloes village lies just inland. It's a place which, despite being situated well away from the coast, has a long seafaring tradition. For many

Wildflowers on the coast

The Deer Park at MARLOES with Skomer in the background

years it was primarily a fishing village and the inhabitants still make a living from the sea, either by fishing for lobster in the coves along St Bride's Bay or by taking visitors out to the nearby islands.

Another less glamorous but equally as lucrative an occupation for the villagers used to be leech gathering. In the days when the creatures were regularly used by doctors Marloes leeches were in great demand. Known as 'Marloes Gulls' the men of the village also once had a fearsome reputation as wreckers, people who set false lights to lure ships onto the rocks. However, there are no recorded instances of deliberate wrecking on this part of the coast and the story is probably little more than an old folk tale.

And talking of folk tales, there is an old tradition in Marloes which involved carrying around a wren, in a large box or bier, on Twelfth Night. A similar custom is often found in other parts of Wales but in Marloes the villagers covered the 'wren house' in ribbons and took it to the houses of their sweethearts. There they sang carols. If the 'wren house' was taken to a house where none of the men had sweethearts the householders would give them beer and send them on their way. The museum at St Fagan's outside Cardiff has an example of a 'wren house' from Marloes dating from 1869 and the custom continued until the early years of the twentieth century.

Nab Head lies north of Marloes, a promontory which was occupied by the hunters and gatherers of the Mesolithic period about 9,000 years ago. This was probably a seasonal settlement but archaeological excavations at the end of the 1970s uncovered almost 4,000 items. Many of these were beads, the production or selling of which may have been a speciality of the settlement. Tower Point is located nearby, offering the visitor a wonderful example of an Iron Age promontory fort.

Further along the coast from Nab Head is the inlet of St Bride's Haven. Whether the haven gave its name to the bay which dominates the coast for the next dozen or so miles, or whether the bay took its name from the inlet, is not known. The identity of St Bride, after whom both of them are named, is equally unclear. It is possible that she could have been St Brigid of Kildare. As St Brigid lived in the sixth century AD and never visited this part of Wales, the use of her name was at best only a dedication.

The present medieval church here has replaced an earlier Christian foundation. The church has a Norman wall and font but most of the building was extensively restored during the Victorian period. Much of the ambience of the place has therefore been lost.

St Bride's Castle overlooks the inlet. It's not really a castle, in the way that Pembroke or Carew are castles, but rather is a large country mansion which was once the home of the Edwards family, the Barons of Kensington. The place is more properly known as Kensington House, after the family, and is now divided into a series of flats for visiting holidaymakers.

Dozens of legends and folk tales exist about this region of Pembrokeshire, probably the least visited part of the Coast Path. The legend of the Ceffyl Dŵr (in English 'water horse') of St Bride's is one of the best-known examples.

According to the story, the water horse was a small but beautiful horse, sometimes dappled grey, sometimes sandy brown. It would suddenly appear and tempt unwary travellers into mounting on its back. The horse would then gallop off, hurling the would-be riders to their deaths. Only ministers of religion, for some strange reason, were allowed to pass on unmolested.

A farmer, working in his fields on the flanks of St Bride's Haven, once supposedly caught the horse and harnessed it to his plough. The horse did not protest and for a while the farmer ploughed on happily. Then, without warning, the horse took to its heels, dragging the farmer and his plough down the field and into the sea. Neither of them were ever seen again.

Another local legend concerns the Tolaeth, phantom knocking or banging which would be heard just before a sudden death. A fisherman from St Bride's once apparently heard the sounds of knocking and the shuffling of feet from the kitchen of his house. For three successive nights he heard the sounds coming from the kitchen.

Several weeks later the fisherman's son was lost at sea. When, eventually, the body was found on the beach it was carried home and the sounds made by the men as they brought it into the kitchen were exactly the same as those heard by the fisherman a few weeks earlier.

There is an old limekiln at St Bride's Haven and two stone coffins which jut out from the earth close to the site of the old chapel. These supposedly date from early Christian times. Some people believe them to be the coffins of fishermen but, really, their origin is unclear. All that is known is that they have been gradually uncovered by erosion over the years.

The rock formations in this area are generally Old Red Sandstone but a little way up the coast, around the Howney Stone, before Little Haven, they change to Pre-Cambrian igneous rocks. These were formed about 650 million years ago. However, due to the movement of the earth's crust, these ancient rocks lie side by side with a series of coal measures, only half the age of the Pre-Cambrian rocks.

Talbenny airfield lies just inland, yet another of the emergency aerodromes established by the RAF

LITTLE HAVEN – more like a Cornish fishing village than a Pembrokeshire seaside town

during the Second World War. Like the other Pembrokeshire bases, Talbenny had a brief life of roaring Merlin engines and dawn missions before relapsing into the quiet solemnity that we find today.

The creeks and inlets on this stretch of the coast have fascinating names, places like Dutch Gin and Brandy Bay – which give a pretty clear indication of what the coves were used for in the seventeenth and eighteenth centuries. The bays are shallow and cut into the coastline like a series of jagged teeth marks. Small wonder that the Revenue cutters based in Pembroke and, later, in Milford Haven – vessels such as the *Speedwell*, *Endeavour* and *Diligence* – had their work cut out to try to stem the flow of illicit goods which poured into the county in the eighteenth century.

The tiny villages of Little Haven and Broad Haven are the most densely populated communities on this part of the coast – if you can use that description about such small, basically seasonal places.

Little Haven remains unspoilt, although it does boast three pubs that are all well used in the summer months. With its narrow lanes and small, attractive cottages the place has a certain similarity to the fishing villages of Cornwall – the residents of Little Haven would undoubtedly say that it is the Cornish villages that are like their community, not the other way around. The similarity is uncanny, however, whichever way you put the emphasis. Even the approach to the place, descending steeply through narrow streets and tiny roads, reminds the visitor, quite clearly, of the distant West Country.

There the comparisons end, however, because Little Haven used to be a coal port. There is no dock and never has been. The coasters and small sailing craft would simply ground themselves on the beach and, at low tide, the coal was loaded across the shingle. Hard as it may be for the modern visitor to believe, Little Haven was once a highly significant port, a vital hub in the Pembrokeshire coal industry.

Broad Haven has been a popular holiday location since the early nineteenth century. By the end of the Victorian age there were bathing machines on these hard sands and crude tin bungalows on the hills above the bay. This was where the wealthy tradesmen and farmers of Haverfordwest and the surrounding countryside came to relax and gain the healthy benefit of sea bathing.

Augustus and Gwen John lived, as children, in Haverfordwest and often came here for their summer holidays. Their father built a house, Rocks Drift, but Tenby in the south of the county proved a more popular spot for the John family. The house is now used as holiday apartments.

The cliffs to the north of the beach were once the site of coalmines, the industry growing and flourishing at the end of the nineteenth century. It is quite possible, however, that mining was carried out at this beach as early as the Middle Ages. Some of the collapsed pits are still visible alongside the Coast Path. These days, Broad Haven is better known for

An early print showing the castle and town of Haverfordwest

its firm sands, its fine sea bathing and its excellent wind surfing.

The town of Haverfordwest lies five miles inland from Broad Haven but, even here, the sea has influenced the development of the community. There was probably an Iron Age settlement in the area as, for many years, this was the ideal place to cross the upper reaches of the Cleddau. After the coming of the Normans, a strong stone castle was built by Gilbert de Clare and the town began to develop as a river port.

King John granted Haverford (the 'west' part of the name was not added until the fifteenth century) the privilege of holding a market and a fair – an important right for the rapidly developing town. The river was a significant link with the wider world and, soon, commodities such as wool, grain and malt were being shipped down the Cleddau and out into the open sea. There was a rich priory here until Henry VIII dissolved the monasteries in the 1530s but it was young William Nichol from the town who achieved religious martyrdom and lasting fame when he was burned at the stake by Mary Tudor in 1558.

Haverfordwest was decimated by bubonic plague in 1653, the population of the town dropping by over a thousand during the course of the epidemic. It was believed that visiting sailors from Milford Haven brought the Black Death to the town. However that might be, for several weeks the smoke of purifying fires, the hollow clatter of church bells and the gruesome instruction to 'Bring out your dead' echoed around a dismal and dispirited community.

It took time but the town recovered, basing its wealth upon the vital sea trade. The remains of old warehouses and quays can still be seen in the lower part of the town, alongside the river which is now largely silted up. The arrival of the railway in 1853 effectively killed off the shipping industry and now the town lies sprawled across the side of a steep hill,

content with its memories. It is full of interesting little streets and fine eighteenth-century buildings. The castle still dominates the town, these days housing the Pembrokeshire Records Office and an interesting local museum.

Haverfordwest is the county town of Pembrokeshire and, as such, plays host to all the usual paraphernalia of local government. Here, also, you will find the headquarters of the Pembrokeshire National Park Authority. The Authority controls and maintains the only true coastal National Park in Britain, now fifty years old. It is a difficult task, one that the Authority has carried out with skill and not a little tact.

The first badge of the PEMBROKESHIRE NATIONAL PARK Authority, now superceded by the new razorbill logo

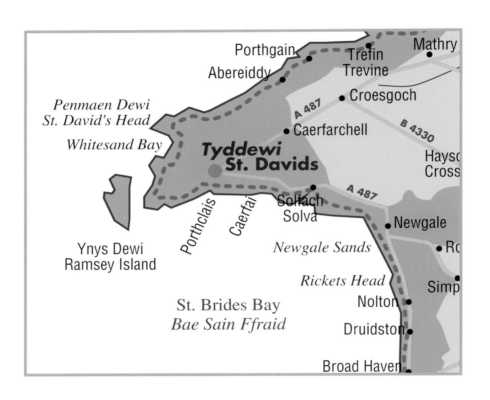

ʙLACK Point lies to the north of Broad Haven beach. It is the site of yet another Iron Age fort but, sadly, this is one which may not be with us much longer. The headland is slipping slowly and irrevocably into the sea. Locals will gleefully tell you that the 'landslide' which began the process was caused by a stray mine being washed ashore and exploding with dire consequences on the rocks in 1944. However, gradual erosion and the timeless working of natural forces are a far more likely cause of the headland's troubles.

The huge chasm to the south-east of the headland is a striking phenomenon. It is a gully or fault which widens every year. Visitors should take time not only to study the fault but also to watch the effortless gliding of the fulmars overhead. The birds often frequent this area and are a spectacular sight as they glide elegantly, easily past.

The cliffs on this stretch of Pembrokeshire coast are cut into coal measures which were formed 300 million years ago. Walk up the shoreline towards Druidstone and Nolton Haven and you will see the measures in the cliff formation. It doesn't take much imagination to see why the area was such a prosperous centre for coal mining back in the nineteenth century.

Nolton Haven was an important harbour for the export of this coal. A mine and several culm pits were situated just inland from here and a tramway once ran down the line of the road towards an embankment which can still be seen between the sea and the road at the Haven. It was here that huge mounds of coal were once stacked to await shipment out of the county.

The largest and most important colliery in the area was Trefran at nearby Newgale. It was founded in the middle years of the nineteenth century and only closed in 1905. Several of the galleries ran out under the sea – literally the western extremity of the South Wales Coalfield.

The anthracite from this pit (like many others in Pembrokeshire) was the hardest and best-burning

The wide expanse of Nᴇᴡɢᴀʟᴇ beach

Clifftop Thrift

coal in the world. The seams here at the extremity of the coalfield were thin and mining eventually became an uneconomical process. However, when Trefran was working, in those halcyon Victorian days, this whole area was a hive of constant activity. Traction engines pulled trolleys or trams stacked high with coal along the coast to Nolton Haven and colliers trudged daily to the pit to plummet down into the earth and then crawl out in narrow tunnels towards the waiting seams of coal. Now only the chimney of the colliery engine house remains, standing tall and defiant at the southern end of Newgale beach.

The beach itself is another of those majestic strips of sand for which Pembrokeshire is justly famous. It stretches for nearly two miles along the coast and is remarkable for the superb storm bank of pebbles and shingle that separates the beach from the adjacent road. This bank was created by rising sea levels and wave action at the end of the Ice Age. Interestingly, the bank includes rocks from as far away as Scotland, carried here by the Irish Sea ice sheet.

The centre of Newgale beach is the point where the Landsker – that mysterious line of demarcation which began at Amroth in the south – finally reaches its conclusion. Although, these days, the Landsker line is invisible, it may once have been a physical bank or stockade as the word Landsker was originally used to describe any ditch or boundary across the land. From Newgale onwards you are in the Welshry. The differences in the people and the culture are obvious, not least in the more common use of the Welsh language on this part of the coast.

At very low tide, perhaps once or twice a year, visitors can see the remains of a sunken forest off the northern end of Newgale beach. Extensive woodlands developed here after the end of the Ice Age, when water levels were much lower than today. Trees such as oak and birch grew here and animals like wolves and foxes scavenged an existence amongst the woodlands. Then the sea levels began to rise, sometimes as fast as ten feet each century, and large areas of the coast were gradually submerged. The sunken forest at Newgale is rarely seen but if you are lucky enough to catch a glimpse of the phenomenon you will be presented with the remains of broken tree stumps and peat beds which are now well over 7,000 years old.

The beach at Newgale is wide open to the elements and severe storms often lash at the sands and pebble bank. The old inn at the centre of the beach used to stand on the seaward side of the road but in 1896 it was washed away by the tide and, thereafter, relocated on the other side of the road.

NEWGALE beach at sunset

Beyond Newgale, the headland of Dinas Fach is a narrow south-facing promontory which has some remarkable caves and yet another ancient fort. Battered by the elements in winter, in the summer months there is no finer place to sit and gaze at the wide expanse of St Bride's Bay.

According to local legend, the adjacent inlet of Porthmynawyd was the scene of dramatic events during the First World War. A German U boat supposedly surfaced offshore and came here to replenish her fresh-water supplies. Whether or not the Royal Navy intercepted the submarine is not recorded but the event has undoubtedly gone down in local folklore.

Brawdy airfield is a few miles inland from here. Established in 1943/4, the base was a Fleet Air Arm station until 1971 and has since played host to the RAF, the American Navy and, latterly, the British Army. For many years Sea King helicopters of the RAF Search & Rescue were based at Brawdy, dozens of climbers, walkers and sailors being helped to safety from the cliffs and sea around the coast. When the RAF pulled out in 1994 the Sea Kings went as well. With the army now in occupation,

Brawdy's runways are no longer required but at least the base remains open, providing much needed revenue for the area.

The village of Solva sits at the seaward end of an ancient glacial melt-water channel, carved out by ice sheets during the Ice Age. When the sea levels subsequently rose, the valley was flooded. It is separated from another glacial valley, the Gwadn, by a narrow ridge known as the Gribin. However, whereas the Solva inlet remains tidal the Gwadn has been silted up for many years. A pleasant sandy beach lies at the mouth of the Gwadn and from here or from the flanking headland there are views of the huge rocks – Black Scar, Green Scar and the Mare – which rear out of the sea just off-shore.

Solva is a pretty village, particularly at high water when the mud and silt of the channel and old harbour are covered by the tide. The village is split into two, Upper and Lower Solva, and it is the lower part of the community that has now become renowned as a boating centre. Here, in the summer months, the yachts and dingies of visitors and locals alike fill the harbour and the cries of the boatpeople or children swimming and diving off the wall of the old quay echo around the inlet. In the seventeenth and eighteenth centuries, however, this was a busy trading port. As late as 1900 there were over 30 ships registered at Solva and a number of warehouses existed to store their cargoes.

Limestone was at the centre of Solva's prosperity and no less than eight limekilns once ran along the shore of the inlet. The limestone was shipped in from quarries at Pembroke and West Williamson and processed at the kilns. The soils of Pembrokeshire have always been full of acid and for many years lime was needed as a fertiliser.

The entrance to Solva harbour is narrow; schooner captains would have had to negotiate a narrow channel between Black Rock and St Elvis Rock in order to deposit their limestone cargo at the quay. The narrow and tidal harbour was only one reason for the eventual decline of limestone trade here – the arrival of the railway in Pembrokeshire in the middle to late nineteenth century was just as influential. The old limekilns still exist but now the only marine industry in Solva comes in the shape of a few locally owned fishing craft.

The port of Solva will always be renowned as the place where Henry Whiteside built the first lighthouse for the Smalls, the series of dangerous rocks and reefs which lie 16 miles to the west of Skomer Island. Whiteside created his fragile lighthouse on the beach at Gwadn in 1775 and then floated it out to the Smalls – in itself a superb feat of

The SMALLS lighthouse sits on its rocky base, several miles offshore

engineering. The lighthouse was an unusual design, having an octagonal upper housing mounted on six wooden and three iron legs.

During a violent storm in the autumn of 1780 one of the Smalls' two lighthouse keepers died. Placed in a wooden box, his body was lashed to the rail of the lighthouse for safety. However, it was three months before the keepers were due to be relieved and in that time the surviving man had gone insane. Since then, Trinity House – until the majority of its lighthouses became automatic – decreed that all lights would be manned by at least three keepers.

Soaring cliffs now lie ahead of any explorer or

Limekilns at SOLVA, empty now but a reminder of a long-forgotten industry

54

visitor. For the next dozen or so miles beyond Solva the vertical or near vertical rock faces seem to soar constantly upwards, as if reaching for the very heavens. For sheer spectacle you will find nothing better anywhere on the Pembrokeshire coast. Here you will discover dozens of fine caves, natural arches, rocky outcrops and blow holes – it is well worth taking time to explore this wonderful and spectacular stretch of coastline.

At Caerbwdi Bay there is an old quarry where the purple sandstone for St Davids Cathedral was once dug out. The quarry was closed for many years but was re-opened in 1972 in order to provide stone for restoration work on the cathedral.

St Non's lies a little further on. Famed as the birthplace of St David, the ruins of the chapel – dedicated to David's mother Non – date from about 1300. There are probably older remains on the site and the standing stones near the chapel are probably the remains of a Bronze Age stone circle, recalling the legend that a large stone protected Non whilst she gave birth. According to legend, a well is supposed to have sprung up on the very spot where David was born, somewhere around the year 500 AD.

The harbour at PORTH CLAIS

Porth Clais has been the harbour serving nearby St Davids for many years. The narrow inlet is a glacial melt-water valley, flooded by the sea (like the inlet at Solva) as the ice retreated about 7,000 years ago. From the sixteenth century onwards, however, this was a busy port, vessels still using the inlet and harbour until the 1960s. In the later days of the port ships brought in coal for the local gas works (now a car park) but for many years limestone was the main commodity. Working limekilns used to stand on the quayside and several of these have now been restored by the National Trust.

Like several other Pembrokeshire towns or villages Porth Clais features in the *Mabinogion*, the ancient Welsh tales of myth, legend and heroic deeds. In the story of Culhwch and Olwen, King Arthur is asked to help Culhwch win the hand of Olwen, daughter of the giant Yspaddaden Pencawr.

Arthur and his knights are set a series of tasks, one of them being to hunt down the giant boar Twrch Trwyth. Transformed into a boar because of his evil deeds, Twrch Trwyth has a comb, razor and shears between his ears and these, along with his tusks, he uses to devastating effect.

Arthur and his knights pursue the boar across Ireland and out into the Irish Sea. He comes ashore at Porth Clais and from here the chase extends to the nearby Preseli Mountains. Several of Arthur's knights are killed in a series of battles before the boar vanishes in the estuary of the River Severn. The rocky outcrops known as Cerrig Marchogion ('the rocks of the knights') on the Preseli Mountains are supposed to mark the graves of the fallen knights.

St Davids lies a mile inland from Porth Clais. This small town or, to be more precise, village was granted official city status in 1995, its famous cathedral being located in the very centre of the community. The smallest city in Britain is devoted to the memory of St David, the first church being built here in the sixth century, around the year AD 550.

ST DAVIDS CATHEDRAL, solemn and atmospheric

The cathedral was destroyed on a number of occasions by raiding Vikings and the present building dates from 1182 when work began under the direction of Bishop Peter de Leia. Long before this, however, St Davids was attracting pilgrims, including significant people like William the Conqueror, from all over Britain.

The cathedral has been modified and rebuilt many times and, consequently, is an amalgamation of many different styles of architecture. It is now the largest cathedral in Wales, sitting virtually hidden from view in a valley alongside the ruined Bishop's Palace. This palace was in disrepair by the mid sixteenth century but its quiet walls and ruined towers are highly atmospheric and are well worth a visit.

Within the cathedral the wonderful latticed oak roof is undoubtedly the building's crowning glory but the unusual monarch's stall and the shrine where the relics of Wales' patron saint are supposedly housed, are also worth attention. Above all, though,

the cathedral is evocative and atmospheric. Nobody who spends time here can fail to be moved by the solemnity of the place – saintliness might be too strong a word but when you combine this cathedral, the Bishop's Palace and the adjacent St Mary's College (dating back to the thirteenth century) this has to be one of the most spiritually powerful locations in the whole of Wales.

The city itself boasts an interesting fifteenth century Celtic Cross and also some intriguing and quiet walks. Here you will find interesting craft and art shops but the town's bookshop, located conveniently close to the cathedral, could be just the place to learn a little more about the man who gave his name to the community. St David lived to a ripe old age, dying it is said on 1st March 588. He was canonised, at the request of Henry I, by Pope Celixtus II some five hundred years later.

In medieval times, two pilgrimages to St Davids Cathedral were accepted as being the equivalent of one to Rome. That, surely, was a sign of the importance of this religious settlement in west Wales – at a time when travel along the roads and coasts of Britain was both uncertain and dangerous!

There are dozens of famous stories about St David and his followers. One of the best concerns his dispute with the Irish chieftain Boia who was encamped close to the settlement of David and his monks. All the attempts of Boia to drive away the religious men came to nothing so he resorted to the age-old tactic of lust. He sent his wife and her handmaidens to dance naked in front of the monks and to taunt them with lewd comments. David and his followers resisted temptation. Eventually, Boia was killed by another warlord and his wife went mad. Clearly it did not pay to meddle with the holy men.

Further along the St Davids peninsula, across Ramsey Sound, lies the rugged, dark and mysterious bulk of Ramsey Island. The tide races through the Sound at speeds of up to 7 knots, making the narrow stretch of water a death trap for the unwary. The jagged stumps of rocks which protrude like broken teeth just off Ramsey, at the narrowest part of the Sound, are the infamous Bitches. They are well named.

Legend will tell you that the Bitches are all that are left of a bridge or causeway that once connected Ramsey to the mainland. St Justinian apparently broke it down because he wanted peace and quiet on the island in which to contemplate and enjoy his 'hair shirted masochism'.

Ramsey Sound has been the scene of many shipwrecks but none is more dramatic or more tragic than the loss of the lifeboat *Gem*. A twelve-oared sailing and pulling boat, the *Gem* set out on 12th October 1910 to assist the ketch *Democrat* which had got into difficulties in the Sound. A heavy sea was running but, despite this, the three crewmen were taken off the *Democrat* and the lifeboat turned for home. However, when trying to manoeuvre through the Bitches, the *Gem* hit the rocks and turned over. Coxswain John Stephens and crewmen James Price and Henry Rowlands were drowned. Fifteen survivors managed to swim to the Bitches where they spent an uncomfortable and often terrifying night before rescue was made by two local boats the following day.

RAMSEY ISLAND, dark and menacing, lies across the Sound from the mainland

The lifeboat *Gem* – lost in RAMSEY SOUND, 1910

Survivors from the *Gem* and *Democrat*, pictured in ST DAVIDS

57

RAMSEY ISLAND seen from Ynys Bery

Ramsey Island has a rough, hilly terrain but, despite this, it was successfully farmed for many years. The island used to belong to the bishop of St Davids and was well stocked with rabbits, sheep and cattle – in addition to producing corn from its own corn mill and water wheel. These days the island has a large colony of grey seals and is also a breeding ground for chough, peregrine falcons, guillemots and fulmars. If you are lucky you may even catch sight of the occasional porpoise. Ramsey is now a nature reserve run by the RSPB but visits and trips around the island can be arranged.

A number of smaller islets and rocks lie off Ramsey. To the south are Ynys Cantwr (the Enchanters Isle), Ynys Bery and Ynys Eilun. They are virtually inaccessible although, many years ago, sheep were sometimes herded and grazed on Ynys Bery. To the north-west are the Bishops and Clerks, the South Bishop Rock with its curiously squat, dumpy lighthouse looking for all the world like a liner at sea. These days the light is fully automatic and the island is a sanctuary for sea birds.

St Justinian is named after the intractable sixth-century religious martyr who lived just across the

RAMSEY ISLAND viewed from the south

The lifeboat station at St Justinian

water on Ramsey. According to legend he constantly berated his followers for their lack of piety and their dubious enthusiasm about life on windswept Ramsey Island. They responded by cutting off his head! The saint had the last word, however, as he simply picked up his decapitated head, put it under his arm and walked across the Sound to St Justinian where he promptly died. His unfaithful followers soon perished from a wide range of horrible and painful diseases.

A ruined chapel marks the site of St Justinian's burial place but perhaps the area is best known for its lifeboat station. This was built in 1911 and has been in constant use ever since. St Justinian is also the place to take a boat trip over the Sound to Ramsey, but only in the summer months.

Glorious WHITESANDS BAY at full tide

The superb sandy beach of Whitesands is backed by extensive dunes and by the rocky crags of Carn Llidi and Carnedd-lleithr. Here you will also find St Davids Golf Club, one of several excellent courses in Pembrokeshire. Overlooking Whitesands Bay, it has superb views and rolling fairways. The beach has strong currents at the north end; this has led the sands to become the best-known surf beach in north Pembrokeshire. The southern part of the beach is more protected and offers fine, safe bathing.

According to legend, St Patrick is said to have embarked from Whitesands Bay for Ireland where, eventually, he became patron saint. There is no proof but many people believe St Patrick to have been a Pembrokeshire man. Certainly he planned to found a religious settlement at St Davids. When told in a vision that the honour of founding such a church had been reserved for another man who would not be born for another thirty years, Patrick merely nodded his agreement and decided to serve God in Ireland instead. Whether or not the story is true, traces of a sixth-century chapel dedicated to St Patrick lie buried beneath the dunes at Whitesands Bay.

This portion of the Pembrokeshire coast is dominated by St Davids Head. Formed 470 million years ago the Ordovician rocks of the headland are harder than the soft sandstone of St Bride's Bay and of the area to the immediate south – hence the prominent headland. The remains of a large Iron Age fort can be found on St Davids Head, three huge stone ramparts literally cutting off the end of the promontory. The foundations of several roundhouses help the visitor to see just how significant an encampment this would have been.

Also out on this headland is a Neolithic burial chamber by the name of Coetan Arthur. The capstone has now collapsed and the visitor needs to remember that in 4000 BC the great stone would have been covered by earth. The chamber remains a fascinating and superb example of a Neolithic cromlech.

A number of rocky outcrops, or tors as they would be called in Devon or Cornwall, run along the northern coast of the peninsula. The first of these is Carn Llidi which backs onto Whitesands Bay. It is closely followed by outcrops like Carn Treliwyd, Carn Perfedd and Penberi. Rugged and stark against the landscape, the outcrops were formed from hard igneous rock many millions of years ago. When the sea levels were higher than they are today, these tors would have been islands, left isolated when the action of the sea wore away or eroded the softer rocks around them.

CARN LLIDI looms over the rocks and coast of Pembrokeshire

The Blue Lagoon

(photo: Philip Clarke)

In the eighteenth and nineteenth centuries Abereiddi used to be a significant slate quarry. The quarry was closed in 1904 and a channel blasted out of the rock to link the old workings to the sea. Now known as the Blue Lagoon, the intention was to create a safe anchorage for the boats of local fishermen. The lagoon remains a striking phenomenon. The colour of the water is often green not blue and is guaranteed to make visitors stop in their tracks and suck in their breath with admiration.

A row of ruined fishermen's cottages, apparently hit by a gigantic wave in 1928, can be found at Abereiddi. If you look closely you can also see the track of the old tramway, which once took slates from the quarry to nearby Porthgain, up on the hill above the cottages.

This is a good area for fossil hunters, one of the few spots along this coast where they can be found – thanks to the great age of the rocks. The slates and shales here are particularly prolific in graptolites.

The harbour of Porthgain was the base for an industrial operation which, until 1932, produced some of the hardest granite ever found. Known as diorite, the stone was used for building and surfacing roads. Here at Porthgain it was crushed and graded in five separate bunkers, then stored in massive hoppers, each of which had a chute for loading ships at the quayside. The hoppers still dominate the harbour.

The harbour entrance at Porthgain

61

PORTHGAIN harbour, once a hive of industry, now peaceful in the sunshine

The company which ran the enterprise, Porthgain Village Industries Ltd, had a fleet of six steam coasters and at one time over a hundred vessels were registered to the port. The coasters were used to export the crushed diorite and also bricks from the nearby brickworks. Originally established to make bricks for the stone-crushing plant, the brickworks quickly became an industry in its own right and was soon exporting its products to places like Llanelli, Bridgewater and Dublin.

Although the quarrying ravaged the immediate area, the land now seems to have reverted to its original shape and form. The stone quarrying ended in 1932 and these days Porthgain is renowned more for its famous Sloop Inn, where the food is always excellent, and for its local artists like Alun Davies than for its industrial heritage.

Quarrying was not the only industry in this part of the world. Until 1918 a mill used to exist at nearby Aberfelin – Archdruid Crwys wrote a famous poem, 'Melin Trefin', about the place. Abercastle was yet another port, so significant that the area was once known as Cwm Badau (the Bay of Boats). Several sailing vessels, each of them between 25 and 30 tons, were built here in the years between 1790 and 1830.

The cliff path between Aberfelin and Abercastle is well worth exploring. The views are spectacular and the cliff top is cut by cracks and erosion – not the

place for those who suffer from vertigo. Pwll Llong is an inaccessible inlet where, in September and October, you might well spot baby seals on the rocks below.

Carreg Samson lies just outside Abercastle. It is a marvellous example of a Neolithic burial chamber or cromlech: legend declares that St Samson put the giant capstone in place using only his little finger. That same finger, says the legend, is buried on Ynys-y-Castell, a small island at the mouth of the inlet leading to Abercastle.

Tiny but fascinating, the beach at ABERCASTLE

The first ever transatlantic telegraph cable was laid from Aber-mawr, at the foot of the Pencaer peninsula, in 1873. You can still see the small building which acted as the terminus for the British end of the cable. These days the beach at Aber-mawr is better known as one of the places to see the purple-blue clays known as Irish Sea till, marine sediments deposited here by the advancing Irish Sea ice sheet some 20,000 years ago.

The sheer cliffs and bulk of the Pencaer Peninsula and Strumble Head now lie ahead of you. This area has always been, and always will be, one of the most spectacular settings in the whole of north Pembrokeshire.

The quiet beach at ABER-MAWR, just one of many deserted strands on the Pembrokeshire coast

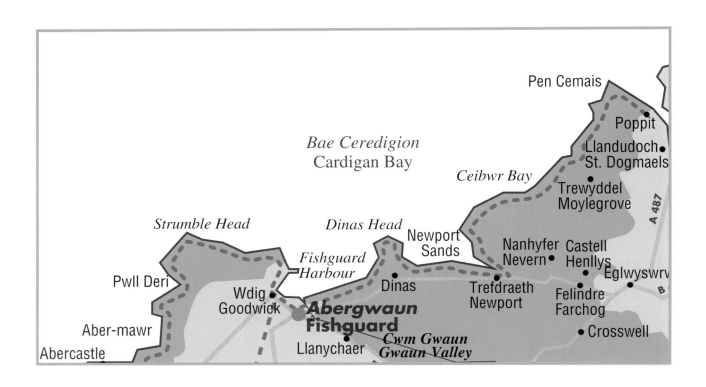

Chapter Six:

Pencaer to Poppit Sands

W HEN the great engineer Isambard Kingdom Brunel came to Fishguard in the course of planning his railway to the west, he took one look at the Pencaer Peninsula and promptly declared

> Pencaer is a barrier thrown by the Ancient God across the path of the Atlantic waves to prevent them separating the land from Fishguard.

He certainly knew what he was talking about. The peninsula sits like a huge clenched fist, defying both the sea and the winds that drive in from the western approaches.

Formed millions of years ago from igneous rocks of the Ordovician period, lava from beneath the sea cooled quickly after an initial eruption to create the massive rock formations that we see today on Strumble Head. There were later eruptions which then deposited more molten lava between and on top of the existing flows. This is known as pillow lava – for fairly obvious reasons!

The climate here is surprisingly mild, regardless of the wind and winter storms. Despite this, the Pencaer Peninsula remains sparsely populated and, as a result, is largely unspoilt.

The cliff scenery on Pencaer is dramatic, sometimes involving sheer drops of up to 400 feet. Wherever there is a sheer cliff you will find rock climbers and this is undoubtedly a climbers' paradise. There are also several Iron Age forts in the area and, of interest to more modern historians, the former home of Desmond Donnelly, one-time MP for Pembrokeshire, at Porth Maen-melyn.

Donnelly was always a 'big' man, someone fated either for the highest office – or for total tragedy. Having backed the wrong horse in the George Brown versus Harold Wilson struggle for supremacy in the Labour Party, Donnelly fell gradually from favour. His political career ended in despair and his life in a confused and partially unexplained spiral of self-destruction.

Strumble Head is famous for its lighthouse. Built in 1907-08, at a cost of approximately £70,000, the light became fully automatic in 1980. Prior to that it was manned by three keepers in what must, surely, have been one of the loneliest postings in Britain. The light flashes four times every 15 seconds

Sea cliffs dominate the PEMBROKESHIRE coast

throughout the day and night. A foghorn, which is heard by shipping five miles away, can also be found here. They have been an invaluable aid to ships and sailors out in the Irish Sea.

This area is renowned for the quality of its bird and marine life. A former Second World War lookout post, situated close to the lighthouse, has been renovated by the National Park Authority and was opened in 1988 as a shelter for bird watchers. A wide range of seabirds frequent the cliffs around the headland but, in particular, in the autumn or early

The isolated lighthouse on STRUMBLE HEAD

winter months this is the ideal location to watch for migratory birds which pause here at the last landfall before the Azores or whichever distant land to where they may be heading.

Above all, though, the Pencaer Peninsula will always be remembered for the dramatic events of February 1797 when 1,400 French soldiers, led by a renegade Irish American called William Tate, landed on Carreg Wastad Point. Britain had been at war with Revolutionary France for several years and the French landing was part of a grander scheme to invade Ireland. The soldiers who landed here, the Legion Noire as the regiment was called, were part of a diversionary force which was originally meant

A puffin stands with outstretched wings, as if drying them in the sun

to come ashore at Bristol. Their task was to cause as much chaos and disaster as possible.

As you would expect with such a 'forlorn hope', the members of the Legion Noire were hardly first-rate troops of the line. They were convicts and the troublemakers from every army in France and many of them still bore the scars of irons on their wrists and ankles. Once they came ashore on the evening of 22nd February 1797 they simply looted the local farmhouses for whatever drink they could find and were soon totally out of the control of their officers.

The invasion lasted just three days but in that time there were a number of clashes between the French and the local inhabitants. One of the most famous concerns a French grenadier who was looting the farmhouse at Brestgarn. Hearing a click from behind him, he assumed it was somebody cocking a pistol, turned and fired a musket ball straight through the face of a grandfather clock. The clock can still be seen at Brestgarn.

The heroine of the hour was Jemima Nicholas, a woman who sometimes acted as a cobbler in Fishguard. Fearing no-one – and certainly not invading Frenchmen – Jemima strode out onto Pencaer and captured twelve enemy soldiers single-handed before declaring that she was going back for more! Local legend will tell you that Lord Cawdor,

The French landing on CARREG WASTAD POINT, a contemporary print from 1797, showing the French ships and soldiers

commander of the British relieving force, persuaded Jemima and other women to march around a nearby hill so that the French would, from a distance, mistake them for guardsmen. In their tall black hats and red shawls it would have been an understandable mistake to make – particularly when the French soldiers were drunk and not seeing very clearly.

Sadly, the story has little credibility. By the time Lord Cawdor arrived at Fishguard on 23rd February it was already dark and visibility was down to under fifty yards. By 9.00 pm that same night Tate, dispirited and depressed by the performance of his troops, had decided to surrender.

The French surrender on GOODWICK SANDS – a fanciful interpretation as no British ships were involved in the episode

The next day the French stacked their arms on Goodwick Beach, below the peninsula, and were marched off into what, for many, would have been welcome captivity. The event had been a farcical affair, one worthy of *Dad's Army* at its best. Yet it has gone down in history as the last time mainland Britain was ever invaded. Another significant outcome of the invasion had very far-reaching effects. Once the news of the landings reached London there was a run on the banks. In those days money was given out in gold and silver and the mighty Bank of England almost ran out of cash. For the first time the Bank had to issue paper promissory notes – the pound note had been born.

The village of Llanwnda lies just inland from Careg Wastad Point. Here you can visit the church (looted and ransacked by the French) and also the actual landing site which is now marked by a memorial stone. The rocky heights of Carnwndda loom over the village. Here the French grenadiers under Irishman Barry St Leger nearly managed to lure Lord Cawdor's troops into an ambush. It was not to be. The whole area is atmospheric, vibrant with the spirit and the sorrow of battles won and battles lost; the sensitive visitor can almost reach out and touch a piece of raw and recent history.

Fishguard is now a quiet country town. Yet two hundred years ago it was an important centre of trade and commerce. Dozens of ships were registered to the port and there were even a few shipbuilding concerns in the area.

Originally a Viking settlement, known as Fisgard, it is easy to see why the sheltered inlet appealed

The memorial stone on CARREG WASTAD POINT, commemorating the French landings in 1797

to these early seafarers. The name Fisgard means 'fish yard' and gives a good indication of why they valued the site. In due course it became one of the most important herring fishing centres in Pembrokeshire. The exporting of commodities like corn, butter and wool simply added to the prosperity of the town.

The harbour at FISHGUARD – a postcard from the beginning of the twentieth century

Take a fast boat to Ireland – from Fishguard, of course

The town's harbour – in reality, based more in the satellite community of Goodwick than Fishguard – was created in 1906. Originally intended as a port to cater for transatlantic passengers, the enterprise was planned to replace Neyland in the south of the county but never really took off. The *Mauritania* called once and there is an interesting tale told about her sister ship, the *Aquitania*. Apparently her captain took one look at the harbour and decided never to use it. The multi-million pound development ground to a halt, almost overnight. Whether or not the story is true, the massive liners of the early twentieth century were certainly too large for the harbour which has only limited space for vessels to manoeuvre around the end of the breakwater and has had to be dredged on many occasions.

Some degree of salvation came in the shape of the Irish Sea ferry trade. As part of the original development a new rail-head had been created at Goodwick – previously a quiet village clinging to the lower slopes of the Pencaer Peninsula – and this soon became an essential component in the ferry service. The trade still continues with regular services being maintained to Rosslare in the Irish Republic.

Fishguard is split into two parts, the modern or upper town which sits on top of a headland, and Lower Fishguard which lies a short distance away at the foot of a steep hill.

Upper Fishguard is a relatively new development, dominated by St Mary's Church where visitors can see the gravestone of invasion heroine Jemima Nicholas. In 1997 a famous tapestry was woven by the women of the town, to commemorate the bicentenary of the invasion. It shows scenes from the landings and is Fishguard's own version of the Bayeaux Tapestry – the 'Over By 'Ere' tapestry as it is sometimes called!! There are also some excellent art and craft shops here and the town is well worth wandering around for a few hours.

The Royal Oak in FISHGUARD – here the French surrendered in 1797

The Royal Oak in the centre of the town was the place where the French and British officers signed the surrender agreement in 1797 although it was not, then, an inn but a simple private house. There is an often made claim that the table on display in the Royal Oak is the very one on which the surrender document was signed. It needs to be taken with a degree of scepticism.

Lower Fishguard is set around a beautiful harbour at the mouth of the Gwaun valley and river. Richard Fenton, author of *A Historical Tour Through Pembrokeshire* – not always most accurate but certainly one of the most entertaining early books on the county – lived here alongside the harbour. The houses remain unspoilt and attractive. It is a pretty spot which featured in the 1971 film

no other than John Paul Jones, founder of the American navy. Sadly this is not true. The man who hove-to off Fishguard, demanding a ransom from the town and the ships in its harbour, was Stephen Mankart. Jones was, at that time, trying the same tactic on the city of Edinburgh.

However, the fort did play a significant part in the invasion of 1797. When he first arrived off Fishguard General Tate sent one of his ships into the harbour to check out the defences and the fort immediately opened fire. The French ship wheeled around and reported to Tate that the town was well defended. Consequently, the French came ashore over the rocks of Carreg Wastad Point rather than the much easier route through the harbour and town.

Fishguard Fort in 1797. Built to protect the town, the cannons had only 3 rounds of ammunition when the French finally arrived

of Dylan Thomas' *Under Milk Wood* which starred Richard Burton, Elizabeth Taylor, Peter O'toole and Ryan Davies.

Fishguard Fort sits on the headland to the north of the lower town. It was built in 1779 after Fishguard was bombarded by a privateer called 'The Black Prince' during the American War of Independence – a classic case of bolting the stable door once the horse had departed! Many people in the area still believe that the captain of the raider was

And the fort? There were only three live rounds of ammunition in the whole place – the shot had been a blank. It has never been clear whether firing the blank shot had been a deliberate ruse or whether the gunners simply mistook the French vessel for a British ship and therefore fired a welcoming salute. Either way, the deception worked. The ruins of the old fort are now maintained by the National Park Authority, the site boasting a battery of restored but original 9 pdr cannon.

Lower Town, FISHGUARD

An idyllic scene, deep in the GWAUN valley

The valley of the Gwaun River was formed as a result of glaciation about 12,000 years ago. The valley was carved out by huge volumes of melt water flowing beneath the ice sheet but the river itself is now little more than a quiet stream. The valley is a beautiful and tranquil area which offers an excellent habitat for animals such as rabbits, badgers and foxes. It remains one of the largest wooded areas in the Pembrokeshire National Park.

Interestingly, New Year's Day is still celebrated here on 13th January. It is a tradition which dates back to 1752 when the Georgian calendar replaced the Julian one. Many dates had to alter but for years valley folk refused to accept the change and continued to measure their year by the old calendar. These days it is a double way of celebrating the New Year.

Many years ago the Gwaun valley was reputed to be full of witches. The belief owes much to the remoteness of the valley but also to the looming Preseli Mountains which lie to the south and imbue the area with a mysterious sense of ancient history. The famous Bluestones at Stonehenge came from nearby Carn Menyn. Weighing up to 4 tons each, their purpose and value, the way they were moved to Wiltshire – and why – remain a mystery that has puzzled historians for years.

Here you will find one of the most famous examples of a Neolithic tomb in the whole of Britain – cromlech Pentre Ifan. Three tall pillars support an enormous capstone which, at its highest point, can easily shelter a rider on horseback. Excavations in 1936 indicated that the barrow was

Cromlech PENTRE IFAN, the most atmospheric of all ancient monuments

originally at least 150 feet long. Local tradition states that this is an excellent spot for seeing fairies, another declaring that if a man fell asleep under the capstone he would either go insane or turn out to be a great poet.

The PRESELI hills in winter

Pentre Ifan is particularly atmospheric and evocative as evening closes in. Stand here at dusk and you will see how easily people conjured creatures such as fairies and goblins out of the shadows which flickered across the stones. As the sun sets over the western sea, only the most insensitive of watchers can fail to feel the hairs rise on the backs of their necks.

At Castell Henllys, close to Eglwyswrw, an Iron Age fort has been excavated – more interestingly, it at all. It may have been cut off by the sea some 8,000 years ago but now it is merely a headland, separated from the mainland by a freshwater marsh. This is a wonderful place to spot razorbills, guillemots and herring gulls which nest on offshore Needle Rock while fulmars and shags can also be seen on the cliffs. As you would expect in such damp conditions, in the spring this whole area is a carpet of bluebells. Sometimes the hawthorn and gorse are so thick that

The reconstructed Iron Age fort at Castell Henllys near EGLWYSWRW

has been reconstructed or rebuilt by archaeologists. The roundhouses have been created out of local materials such as wood, wattle and daub and offer a superb experience for the visitor. Come here on a wet afternoon in autumn and you will surely gain a great insight into life in an Iron Age village all those centuries ago. The National Park Authority now owns Castell Henllys.

To the north lies Dinas Island, not really an island you can only walk along the tracks and pathway with the greatest of difficulty.

In the Middle Ages the ancient game of Cnapan, a forerunner of rugby, was widely played along this stretch of coast. Played with a hard wooden ball, the opposing teams sometimes consisted of hundreds of players. Whole villages would compete against each other, many of them on horseback, with the game covering large sections of the countryside and often lasting for several days. Injuries were frequent, hardly surprising when heavy cudgels or clubs were used by many players. The writer George Owen described Cnapan in his *Description of Pembrokeshire* which was published in 1603. Owen often played the game and on at least one occasion sustained serious injuries in a match.

Newport is an ancient Marcher township, founded about the year 1200 by the lord of Cemais. The town is unusual in that it is a genuine Norman borough set in the very heart of the Welshry. The castle at the centre of the town was twice destroyed by attacking Welsh forces and after the thirteenth century it was replaced by a strong stone fortress. By the sixteenth century the castle was in ruins but was then restored by the Owen family and, later, a comfortable residence was created in the gatehouse.

The town became an important trading centre, importing goods across the sands of the Parrog – once a separate community but now part of Newport itself. Coal and culm were still coming ashore here as late as the 1930s. These days Newport is a busy little community, particularly in the summer months, and has a wealth of gift shops where the visitor can while away an hour or so.

The beach at Parrog is part of the Nevern Estuary but it is rocky and full of shingle when the tide is full. Only at low tide is sand revealed. The beach at Newport (Traeth Mawr as it is called, the 'Big Beach') has to be one of the finest strips of sand on the whole of the Pembrokeshire north coast and is ideal for swimming and boating.

Newport Golf Club overlooks Traeth Mawr. The course is reckoned by connoisseurs to be one of the best links courses in Wales, even though it has only 9 holes. The views from the fairways are stunning and when the wind blows from the sea the course will test even the most talented of golfers. The clubhouse, incidentally, welcomes visitors – good food, good conversation and a great atmosphere. What more could you want?

The dunes at Newport, below the golf course, have suffered from overuse by the public but planting of marram grass by the National Park Authority has stabilised the erosion. Take time to explore the estuary, beach and sand dunes as here you will find dozens of wading birds and, hopefully, an elegant heron or two as well.

The Witches Cauldron is a collapsed cave on the Coastal Path close to Ceibwr Bay – one of the best blow holes on the Pembrokeshire coast. There are a number of inlets and outlets in the cave and to

NEWPORT SANDS, deserted and calm on a bright morning

watch from above as a rough sea sweeps through the openings and channel is an experience not to be missed.

The cliff scenery beyond Newport is spectacular. The rocks are made up of alternating layers of sandstone and mudstone created by underwater landslides 450 million years ago. When the layers of sand and mud were later compressed by the collision of continents it produced the folds which are now

Cemaes Head soars upwards for nearly 600 feet. Much of this headland is now a nature reserve, owned and run by the Wildlife Trust South and West Wales. Guillemots, fulmars and cormorants frequent the cliffs, as do choughs which, although rare in many parts of Britain, seem to thrive in Pembrokeshire. A scheme involving the Wildlife Trust South and West Wales and the National Park Authority has recently introduced ponies to graze

The cliffs at CEIBWR

clearly visible in the cliffs between Ceibwr Bay and Cemaes Head.

The wind can be fearsome on this stretch of coast. A wonderful story tells of a henhouse belonging to one cliff-top dwelling which was lifted by the wind and carried for 200 yards before being deposited in the next field. The hens continued to cluck happily and next morning laid their eggs as if nothing had happened!

on the cliff-tops. This will improve the quality of the grass on these windswept cliffs and thus greatly help the survival prospects of the choughs.

And so to Poppit Sands at the mouth of the River Teifi. Sand dunes and golden beaches line the river which winds its way back inland towards the town of Cardigan. On a fine day you should be able to pick out Cader Idris, many miles to the north, as well as Cardigan Island which is now a nature reserve.

The steamer *Herefordshire* was wrecked on the island in 1934, breaking free from her tugs as she was being towed to the Clyde for scrapping. Rats from the aged liner escaped onto the island, much to the detriment of the bird colonies. In 1968 over a thousand rodents were killed off by Warfarin experiments and the birds began to return.

Poppit Sands marks the end of the Pembrokeshire coast. From here on, the county of Ceredigion takes over – no less interesting, no less full of history, legend and fascinating fact than that to be found in the area to the south. However, it is not Pembrokeshire and as far as Ceredigion is concerned – well, as the man once said, that is another story.

Planting marram grass at POPPIT SANDS

Select Bibliography

Phil Carradice – *The Last Invasion*, Village
  Publishing, 1992
Phil Carradice – *The Book of Pembroke Dock*,
  Barracuda Books, 1990
Phil Carradice – *Pembroke: For King & Parliament*,
  Pembroke Town Council, 1992
Phil Carradice – *Welsh Islands*, Barracuda Books,
  1997
Paul Davis – *A Company of Forts: A Guide to the
  Medieval Castles of West Wales*, Gomer, 2000
Malcolm Easton & Romilly John – *Augustus John*,
  HMSO, 1975
Sybil Edwards – *The Story of the Milford Haven
  Waterway*, Logaston Press, 2001
John Evans – *Flying Boat Haven*, Aviation &
  Maritime Research, 1985
John Fenna – *Discovering Pembrokeshire by Bicycle*,
  Gomer, 2000
F P Gwynne – *Allen's Guide to Tenby*, Kent & Co,
  1890
Roscoe Howells – *Pembrokeshire's Islands*, Gomer,
  1994
Wendy Hughes – *The Story of Pembrokeshire*, Gwasg
  Carreg Gwalch, 1993
Brian John – *Pembrokeshire Past & Present*, Greencroft
  Books, 1995
Alan Reid – *The Castles of Wales*, Letts Guides, 1973
Tony Roberts – *Myths & Legends of Pembrokeshire*,
  Pembs Handbooks, 1974
Patrick Stark – *Walking the Pembrokeshire Coast Path*,
  Gomer, 1990

Place-names which have English and Welsh forms, both of which are in current use.

English form	Welsh form	English form	Welsh form
Brawdy	Breudeth	Newport	Trefdraeth
Caldey Island	Ynys Bŷr	Pembroke	Penfro
Cardigan	Aberteifi	Pembroke Dock	Doc Penfro
Fishguard	Abergwaun	Pembrokeshire	Sir Benfro
Goodwick	Wdig	Pendine	Pentywyn
Haverfordwest	Hwlffordd	Ramsey Island	Ynys Dewi
Laugharne	Talacharn	St Bride's Haven	Bae Sain Ffred
Lower Fishguard	Cwm Abergwaun	St Davids	Tyddewi
Manorbier	Maenorbŷr	St David's Head	Penmaendewi
Milford Haven	Aberdaugleddau	Solva	Solfach
Narberth	Arberth	Tenby	Dinbych-y-pysgod
		Whitesands	Traeth Mawr